6.95
L

HOW
TO BUY
AT
AUCTION

by Michael De Forrest

SIMON AND SCHUSTER • NEW YORK

FIRST PRINTING

SBN 671-21172-2
Library of Congress Catalog Card Number: 76-188500
Designed by Irving Perkins
Manufactured in the United States of America
By The Book Press, Brattleboro, Vt.

To BETTY, WHO HELPED MOST, AND TO
THE MANY HONEST AUCTIONEERS WHO TAUGHT
ME SO MUCH, AND TO THE DISHONEST ONES
FROM WHOM I LEARNED EVEN MORE.

CONTENTS

signor's reserve • The order bid • Withdrawing a bid • Multi-item lots • There aren't any friends at auction

HOW TO BUY
AT AUCTION

1 WHY TO BUY AT AUCTION

EVERYTHING THAT man has ever needed, wanted, eaten, drunk, inhabited, worn, admired or enjoyed, and a good many things that he ultimately has not enjoyed, has at one time or another, in one place or another, been sold at auction. And that is one of the best reasons for auction attendance. The incredible variety of the lots that you will have an opportunity to consider through two or three diversified auction sessions might otherwise be found only through months—perhaps years—of patient, relentless browsing and shopping. Many rare or unique lots, of course, are available to the public through no other channel. At auction, you may be offered anything from junk to jewels in the course of a single session. Sometimes, in fact, you will find the latter put up for sale in the guise of the former. Which suggests an additional reason—perhaps the most tantalizing—for buying at auction: the possibility of making a "find."

Does that word "everything" seem to be an exaggerated claim? Well, do a little digging and you will quickly agree that it is hard to find anything that hasn't been put up for auction. Herodotus wrote about an auction of brides in ancient Babylon. After the beauties had been sold, the ugly and deformed were disposed of to whoever would accept the smallest dowry for taking them away—a feature of the auction that D. W. Griffith dramatized in an episode of his film *Intolerance*. Samuel Pepys's diary includes a description of a seventeenth-century auction at which the lots included three sailing ships. George Washington was an avid auction buyer, and acquired some of the furnishings for Mount Vernon at the sale of a neighbor's estate. Auction lists indicate that Washington also bought some lots of bottles—for use, no doubt, in decanting his famous homemade wine. Wine, for that matter, currently enjoys collectable status and goes up for auction in lots of outstanding vintage. Flowers, fruit, fish and furs are auctioned to processors and distributors. Art, antiques and automobiles pass under the auctioneer's hammer. So do meats, machines and movie cameras. Tournament golfers have been sold to the highest bidder at Calcutta auctions, in which the successful buyer owns the player for the tournament period and claims his share of the purse. But the most extraordinary auction on record was the sale at which Marcus Didius Salvius Julianus bought the whole of the Roman Empire with a bid of 25,000 sesterces. And that was in A.D. 193, when Roman rule extended from Asia Minor west through Europe all the way to Britain. A not inconsequential auction lot, wouldn't you agree? In a sense, Didius had managed to acquire for himself the Imperial title to much of the known world. His triumph, however, was astonishingly brief. If you look up Didius Julianus in your encyclopedia, you will find that the year of his acquisition of the throne is also the year of his death— since, some months later, the Praetorians, who had put the empire on the auction block, took it upon themselves to relieve the lucky bidder of his purchase.

Not in the market for an empire? Or perhaps you think it unfair to cite as an example an auction that took place in the year 193? Then how about an auction lot consisting of the original ruby slippers in which Judy Garland skipped down the yellow brick road to the emerald city of Oz? Or the big brass bed of which "The Unsinkable Molly Brown" frequently sang? Interested in buying *Le Cyprès et L'Arbre en Fleurs,* a late painting by Van Gogh? Or a 69.42-carat pear-shaped diamond? A footed narcissus bowl in lavender porcelain of the Sung Dynasty? Twenty-six pages from the First Folio of the works of Shakespeare? Or the second printed draft of the Constitution of the United States, annotated during the proceedings of the Federal Convention by Pierce Butler, delegate from South Carolina? A 1926 Rolls-Royce Silver Ghost roadster? All of these items were sold at recent auctions. And at prices, perhaps, not far removed from the sum Didius forked over for his empire. The Van Gogh brought $1,300,000 at Parke-Bernet's record-breaking sale of Impressionist paintings. Miss Garland's "Dorothy" slippers fetched a trim $15,000 at the eighteen-day auction series in which the David Weisz Company disposed of a multitude of properties, furnishings and costumes from the Metro-Goldwyn-Mayer film studios. Molly Brown's big brass bed pulled $3,000 at the same sale. The draft of the Constitution went for $160,000 at Parke-Bernet. The R-R 1926 roadster, for $10,000. The leaves from the First Folio Shakespeare earned $700. Also at Parke-Bernet, the narcissus bowl brought $110,400, establishing a new world-record price for a piece of pottery or porcelain sold at auction. As for the 69.42-carat diamond, it was, of course, the Cartier diamond, which Mr. Richard Burton, his agent having dropped out when the bidding at the Parke-Bernet sale reached $1,000,000, later purchased privately from Cartier, the successful auction bidder at $1,050,000. In the financial, entertainment and fashion pages of the nation's newspapers, there was considerable speculation as to how much it had cost Mr. Burton not to have purchased the jewel at auction. Economy—about which more later—is another splendid reason for you and me to buy at auction.

But let us come down from the stratosphere of fine art and fabulous jewels and movie-star memorabilia, and look at the incredible variety of auction items that don't make headlines, don't set new price records, don't inspire three of the world's wealthiest men and the directors of four of the nation's major museums to sit in competition. Maybe you're only looking for a new sofa for your living room.

That is what we were doing when the auction bug first bit. Every sofa we saw that we wanted cost more than we could afford to pay. And every ugly piece that did fit our budget scored points for that alone. Auction sales, we then believed, were largely matters of works of art that sold for considerable fortunes in plush galleries, or carnival goods, shabby rugs and cheap cameras put up in smoky, glaringly lighted stores where Times Square sharpies shouted bids over deafening speaker systems. Somewhere between those extremes, we conceded a place to the rural auctioneer presiding over the sale of old stoneware crocks and rusted household equipment and farm implements. Accompanying this quite limited vision was the remembered chant of the tobacco auctioneer whose radio spots for the American Tobacco Company concluded with the commercial's only two intelligible words: "Sold American." Out of that, try to conjure an acceptable piece of furniture successfully bid and you'll understand why we hadn't thought of trying to buy that sofa at an auction sale.

A friend of mine maintains that one reason movies are so much better than real life is that in a film you always know when the important moments are coming because the music clues you in. And it is true that the quiet of that Sunday morning when Betty turned a page of *The New York Times* and looked up and said, "Oh, look, they're having an auction to sell off the furniture from the World's Fair . . ." was unbroken by fanfares or flourishes. There was only the crisp snap of the newspaper being folded open at that page. Hardly compelling enough to suggest that we were about to turn a corner that would lead us not only to the long-sought-for sofa, but also to a new hobby that would eventually become an important element in our life.

I don't think either of us had ever attended an auction sale before. And we probably would not have gone to that one if it had not been that the location and the hours of exhibition made it possible for me to attend the inspection on my way to work the morning of the sale. I told Betty that I would go with her to look around, but that she would be on her own when the sale began later that morning. She said that she would probably be afraid to bid, and I think it very likely that she was, although it will soon become apparent that she somehow managed to conquer that fear.

The fair having closed the year before, the contents of the various administration buildings were being sold. We inched along aisles of desks and file cabinets, negotiated jungles of upended chairs and towers of stacked wastebaskets, picked our way through rooms carpeted with typewriters, dictaphones, adding machines. And there, in one of the executive offices, was *the* sofa, looking as unused as a sample in a designer's showroom. Immaculately upholstered in soft gray tweed, floating on a beautifully crafted six-legged frame of gleaming chrome. Betty and I turned to each other, nodded, and tried hard to memorize the number on the white tag pinned to the cushion. (It was our first time out, remember, and we hadn't even thought to take along a notebook. *See Chapter 3: How to Inspect an Auction.*) If catalogues there were, we were too green to ask for one. And to make matters worse—and yet, in a way, better—our inspection turned up a pair of terrific chairs and a coffee table that provided us with three more three-digit numbers on which to concentrate, while other offices revealed sofas and chairs with numbers confusingly close to those on the lots we wanted. "Let's go for coffee," I said.

In the coffee shop, we borrowed a pencil from the waitress and kind of half-stabbed, half-tore those important lot numbers onto a paper napkin. The logical conclusion to this adventure would be that we wound up either with nothing, or with several lots that we hadn't wanted instead of the pieces that we liked. But as it turned out, most of the buyers that day were dealers in office equipment and business machines, and while file cabinets, typewriters, wastebaskets and metal desks drew competitive bidding, the upholstered furniture, the draperies and decorations and the two automobiles that had been included in the sale got the kind of quick knocks that delight buyers. The next day a truckman delivered the sofa, the two chairs and the coffee table, plus a teakwood occasional table, an enormous credenza and a small chest of drawers, which we had also won. The night before, Betty had brought home two pairs of custom-made draperies that she had, on impulse, successfully bid in at $5. Altogether, the lots we purchased at that auction cost us less than $600, including the truckman's charge. This was about one-fifth the retail value of the identical items, and perhaps half what they would have cost in a secondhand store, provided they could have been found in comparable condition in a used-furniture shop. Of course they weren't, technically, new, but not one of them showed a sign of wear. In fact, we're still using all of them.

Which brings me back to one of the best of all reasons for buying at auction: not only will you have an opportunity to purchase an incredible variety of items, many of which would otherwise be unavailable, but also, you should be able to save at least one-third on the retail purchase price when you do. How much more you can save will depend on your ingenuity and patience, the canniness of your competition and the shrewdness of the auctioneer. Countless other factors also can affect auction prices—the weather (smart buyers pray for rain and snow as fervently as auctioneers hope for a fine day), the stock market (a bearish market will depress prices on lots in the middle range; a bullish trend can set them soaring right straight up the line), the location of the sale (big furniture will go begging in some areas, bric-a-brac, in others, where, if you buy against the trend, you can make some fine purchases*), the nature of the auction (the announcement of the sale of an estate of a well-known collector will sound the call to battle for other collectors and dealers, and prices will rise accordingly), the date of the sale (in suburbia and beyond, holidays are popular auction dates for the excellent reason that crowds are usually larger and spirits—and bids—observably higher).

There are seasonal variations in auction prices too, with what the dealers call "more realistic" (translation: lower) prices generally prevailing at metropolitan auctions held in midsummer, when many of the wealthier private buyers are out of the city and dealer competition is reduced by seasonal slowness and summer travel. Midsummer prices at country sales, on the other hand, particularly in resort areas where vacationers and summer residents swell the crowd, are apt to go substantially beyond the amounts comparable lots bring at fall and winter sales. Smaller crowds usually result in lower prices at auction, making your willingness to go against seasonal trends another factor in buying economically.

But even on a fine holiday afternoon, with the stock market

---

* At a country auction in Pennsylvania, I bid in a brass bed at $17. In the New York City area, a similar bed brings $50 and up-up-up. There are exceptions, but furniture usually brings less at rural sales than it does in the city. One exception: massive pieces that most city apartment dwellers are obliged to forgo. If you happen to be looking for one of those great, baronial dining-room sets, scout the metropolitan auction rooms for an occasionally astonishing buy. If you're in search of a rolltop desk or a round oak table—as everyone currently seems to be—hit the back roads (*see Chapter 2: How to Find an Auction*) in search of a country auction.

in a confidently bullish phase, in city or country, you can still buy what you want for considerably less than you would pay elsewhere, if you know how to buy at auction.

Although many of the lots purchased at auction are bought on impulse, and that is part, but only part, of the fun—which brings us to another good reason for buying at auction: *it is fun*; more fun, I think, than any other method of shopping— your major auction buys will actually be among the most carefully considered purchases that you will ever make. For one thing, you will be establishing the selling price of any lot that you successfully bid in. And you will have taken into consideration not only the estimated value of the item, but its potential worth to *you*—which may actually have no close relation to the value of the article, particularly if it completes a set or enriches a collection. You will have asked yourself whether or not you would walk into a retail shop and buy the identical article for the same amount at which you set your maximum bid. You will have determined in advance how you want to use it, knowing that articles bought at auction generally are not returnable. For that same reason, you will have examined it much more carefully than you would probably inspect a floor sample in a department store.* In short, you will be making an informed purchase, which any consumer expert will tell you is the most important factor in buying economically.

Economy has nothing to do with those legendary "finds" that people will immediately start telling you they've made as

* You will also be glad to remember that the article you inspect at the auction exhibition is the article that you will receive. No wrong models delivered from the manufacturer's warehouse. No frustrating little postcards telling you that your merchandise is out of stock and won't be available for at least three weeks. No disappointing wrong colors, or undelivered parts. You will receive what you see at the exhibition, *as* you see it, and you will probably want to (have to) remove it immediately at the conclusion of the sale. These fairly constant rules of auction demand some responsibility of the buyer, but they are not without some comforting aspects.

soon as they learn of your interest in auctions. (*See Chapter 5: How to Make a Killing.*) Buying economically involves purchasing something that you can enjoy using, and paying less than it would cost if you did not buy it at auction. Something worth $200 that you purchase for $125. Or for $50. If you bought it for less—for $20, or even for $1*—you probably ought to consider that you have made a find, which is one of the nicest things that can happen when you buy at auction. Obviously, not everything that you buy is going to be a treasure. You should expect to save at least one-third on your auction-bought items, even as you expect to pay less for your meal in a cafeteria, less for your groceries in a supermarket, less for your appliances at a discount house. And it will become apparent that there are countless instances in which your auction savings will be considerably in excess of $33\frac{1}{3}$ percent off retail.

Equally important, though, is the enjoyment of buying at auction. There really isn't anything exactly like it. At a major sale, the excitement might be compared to that of a neck-and-neck race down the homestretch in the Kentucky Derby. Breathtaking is the only word for the kind of suspense generated by the fast exchange of bids on an important lot. And even if the level is far short of the thousands, or hundreds of thousands—if you are involved in the bidding, no matter how cool you try to play it, you're going to succumb to the exhilarating tension that is symptomatic of what some people call "auction fever." It can be devastating or delightful, depending entirely on how you handle it. It is persistent but, fortunately, not known to be fatal. Bidding at auction com-

---

* Once I found a beautiful Chippendale blanket chest that I picked up for $20 at the end of a long, otherwise unrewarding auction. Our $1 find was an Oriental Export Ware dish that Betty bought in a mixed lot of saucers, odd plates and bottles. An antiques shop in New York offers a comparable plate for $200. These examples are not tossed in to prove how brilliant we are, but to indicate that there are still some "finds" to be made.

bines some of the heady excitement of the gambling tables with the bold strategy of an audacious investment in the stock market. It offers you an opportunity to be daring in a situation of protected peril: for if you have carefully inspected the auction lots, and do not too greatly exceed your established maximum bids, you cannot—indeed you *will* not—be hurt too badly. There's satisfaction, too, in being able to perceive the intentions of your opponents, and to apply that information to your advantage. If you can also "read" the auctioneer —and you might be able to after attending even one or two of his sales—you're in a splendid position to buy wisely and to have a fine time doing it. At an auction sale, a keen understanding of human nature and a sharply perceptive eye and ear are worth more than an unlimited supply of cash.

You will have sufficient funds, of course, to cover your bids, but beyond that, one of the best features of auction buying is that you don't need to spend wildly in order to bid successfully. Very few buyers bid recklessly, with that devil-may-care, caution-to-the-winds, money-is-no-object abandon. They get hurt too many times, too quickly, and either learn to bid more realistically or retire from the auction scene. Your most important competitors will probably have set a maximum bid on each lot in which they are interested. If you are willing to top that by one bid—or even if you can successfully convince them that you *intend* to top *any* bid, while at the same time subtly suggesting to the auctioneer that you are about to drop out at any moment—you stand a good chance of taking the lot.

At a legitimate auction (and we will discuss those that are not—because, let's face it, some auctions *aren't*, although they constitute a surprisingly small minority), remember, it is the buyer who sets the price. *You* are the only one who can determine how much you are willing to pay for an item. You are, in a sense, helping to establish its value and, indirectly, the value of related items. When one work by an artist suddenly soars to an unexpectedly high auction price, dealers go back to their galleries and make similar increases in their prices for other works by that painter. And not infrequently an important collector will be persuaded to part with a treasure from his collection with "Look what we realized on the ———— at that last sale! And yours is an even more significant work!"

For the last few years, decorative glass, bronzes and leaded glass lampshades made by Louis Comfort Tiffany have been bringing increasingly high prices, with the result that more and more Tiffany items are finding their way to the auction block, while shopkeepers have a busy time keeping their prices in line with those prevailing at auction. In a year's auction attendance, it is now quite possible to sit before several hundred Tiffany pieces. It is, in fact, possible to sit before the same piece at several different sales—dealers picking up an item at one auction for the purpose of placing it on sale at another and realizing a tidy profit for their pains. In many cases, the proprietors of smaller antiques shops have disposed of their Tiffany pieces by giving them over to an auctioneer, who can offer them to a larger clientele at sales where supply and demand will combine with the excitement of competition to inspire still further price increases. This will no doubt continue—with a leveling off eventually if the bidders finally decide that they have had enough.

If the consignor sets too high a reserve on an item, the sale can fail. If the auctioneer demands a too-high opening bid, the lot may have to be passed. A salesroom packed with shills cannot successfully move a single item. Only you, as an active, informed bidder, can establish a valid selling price for an item. You are, consequently, in an infinitely better bargaining position than you would occupy at any other kind of sale. Most auctioneers know this, but succeed to the degree to which they manage to ignore it.

Very few potential buyers, however, are aware of the

strength of their position. This is not to suggest that you will win every lot on which you set a maximum bid. You won't. And if you expect to, you will be sorely disappointed. But one of the joys of buying at auction is the awareness that in a few minutes there will be another lot put up for bids. That in a few days, or weeks, there will be another auction to inspect, another sale to attend—with, perhaps, even more exciting lots to be considered. In time, the lots that you missed will no longer haunt you, while the items that you successfully bid in will continue to delight you and to remind you of the skill with which you bought at auction.

You can learn a lot at auction, too. Visiting the exhibition of an important auction can be more informative than ten museum tours. For one thing, the auction exhibition will be far more concentrated—from a few to, at the most, a few hundred lots. You will consequently devote more time and attention to the things that you inspect. When I go to a museum, I always promise myself that I'll visit only one or two rooms, but invariably my eye is attracted by something in another gallery, and I think it would be a shame to leave without taking at least another look at a particular favorite, and before I know it, my limited visit has spontaneously expanded into still another general tour. At an auction exhibition, on the other hand, I may look at only ten paintings. At only seven works of sculpture. At only a few really important porcelains. At, perhaps, twenty pieces of fine furniture, any one of which might deserve a place in a museum. And even more important, at the auction exhibition I have an opportunity to examine these items. To get close to them. To handle them (carefully). To see how they are made. How they feel. Where they are signed. To involve myself with them in ways that no museum would permit.

Any expert will tell you that this kind of investigation is the best possible path to knowing and appreciating fine things. It is a privilege most auction galleries will grant you. Take advantage of it. But don't abuse it. Show the item under consideration the kind of respect that it merits. You will never learn very much beyond what the bottoms of a lot of things look like if you just go busily about turning everything upside down and looking at its underside. (And hold the top down when you do. Train yourself to do this automatically. You will save yourself a lot of embarrassment and possibly some occasional breakage. You will also show the attendant—he is watching you with suspicion, whether or not you are aware of it—that you know how to handle things as they should be handled. Hold closed the tops of inkwells, the covers of boxes, the lids of jars, the stoppers in bottles. Hold hinged items so that they remain shut. Does this seem too ridiculously elementary? Do it anyway! Do not lift mugs, cups, pitchers, sugar bowls, biscuit jars, vegetable dishes, tureens, decanters, coffeepots, teapots, chocolate pots, or anything else of pottery, porcelain or glass, by the handle[s]. You are there to inspect things, you know, not to break them. If a handle is cracked, or has been repaired, it might not sustain the weight of the article. Standing with a delicate porcelain ear clutched in one hand and a wreath of broken china at your feet is, at best, an unbecoming pose. Avoid it. Don't try to lift marble or bronze or any other item that suggests it might be too heavy or awkward for you to handle. Ask the attendant to do it for you. *Then* look at its underside, if that's part of your search for information.)

Apply yourself to the items that interest you. Look at them closely. Examine them carefully. Compare the pieces with their catalogue descriptions. If the auctioneer or one of the gallery attendants is available and you have specific questions about a particular item, you can learn still more by listening to the answers.

"What do you think this will go for?" will probably be what

you most want to ask, and it is probably the last thing you ought to bother to ask most auctioneers. Some of them really don't know. Others simply will not say. A few, in the interest of stimulating higher bidding, will double or triple the sum that they actually expect to realize. (In which case, even if you aren't inspired to increase the amount of your bid, you will undoubtedly be impressed by what will appear to have been a fantastic bargain. This, in turn, will encourage you to bid more freely on other lots.) Such answers contribute to the accumulation of a good deal of useless information and confusion. I know some gentlemen who can, and will, accurately answer this question within a few dollars of the amount of the successful bid. These reliable informants, however, are not in the majority, and—let's face it—not even the most experienced auctioneer knows what will happen once the bidding begins.*

That's another reason auction sales can be such fun. If you want to learn about prices, attend the sale session—and take notes. But go to the exhibition if you want to develop the kind of eye that will lead you to fine items of quality and value; if you would like to sharpen that sixth sense of yours, so that

---

* A celebrated actress who has been known to acquire a trinket or two— including some of the world's most fabled jewels—at auction once consigned a painting from her collection for sale via a gallery at which a work by the same artist had previously realized about $500,000. Since the actress' painting was in every respect as fine as the work that had preceded it to the auction block, it was expected to bring an equivalent amount. When the bidding closed somewhere short of one-tenth of that figure, the painting was bid in by the auctioneer and bought back for the owner. Yet a thoroughly responsible advance estimate would have predicted a selling price for the picture of something close to $500,000. On a somewhat less exalted level, we recently watched a small, attractive bentwood whatnot climb to $250, much to the laughing amazement of the auctioneer, who had expected the piece to bring, perhaps, $75 or, with a bit of pressure, $100. But two bidders got carried away, and one of them carried away her prize, to the auctioneer's cheerful applause. Occasionally I have heard an auctioneer, surprised by the sudden escalation of bids, blurt out, "It isn't worth it!" but only when the fires of competition were sufficiently out of control to yield to no damper.

intuition is supported by information; if you would enjoy having a bit of your own easy expertise to draw upon. You will be amazed at how much you will learn, how much fun you will have, how much money you can save, and how many treasures you can collect as you bid and buy at auction.

2 HOW TO FIND AN AUCTION

AFTER THAT first sale, which furnished our living room, we picked up quite a few inexpensive things—dishes and glasses, a clock that didn't run (and still doesn't, although it has been in the repair shop for at least half the time that we have owned it), woodenware, old salt-glaze pottery, chipped crocks and jugs (they *looked* old), greasy oil lamps (they *were* old) and other unimportant lots from neighborhood auctions. At that time, an hour seemed like a long drive to an auction, and I suppose it was if it led to nothing more important than a cracked stoneware crock in which someone had once put up pickles. We bought a lot of old yellow bowls, too—the big, roomy kind in which my grandmother used to make bread. In short, we bought cheap. If a lot was about to be knocked down at $2, we would hasten to bid it in at $3, without ever stopping to ask ourselves why it might have been going at $2. (Ninety-nine times out of a hundred, the answer is undesirability. The hundredth time, it just might have been a piece of eighteenth-century creamware that everyone else thought undesirable, but that would bring $50 in an antiques shop.)

Bright reproductions of old bottles glittered on our window-sills. Jugs and crocks stood like sentinels guarding the front and back steps of our house. Yellow pottery bowls and gray-blue ginger jars looked fresh and charming holding bunches of daisies. Wooden troughs became fruit bowls and bread trays. On Thanksgiving, our table looked mighty like a spread in a women's magazine. Throughout the other 364 days of the year, however, that constantly intensifying country-kitchen effect was getting to be a bit much. One piece of primitive earthenware might add a mellow note to the austere chrome and tweed of our ultramodern sofa. But three . . . six . . . seven (including a big redware churn in which we kept ceiling-high arrangements of foliage) soon silently advised us that our auction attendance was taking us too far in one direction and, literally, not far enough in another. "What we need to do," Betty said, "is find an auction where they don't sell yellow crockery." Obviously, the time had come for us to enlarge our sphere of auction activity.

But in what direction?

Although held within the densely packed suburbs of New York City, the auctions that we had been attending were typical country sales. Someone was moving. A hardware store was going out of business.* An old house was being torn down. There had been a death in the family. The owner of an antiques shop was retiring, or needed to raise cash, or wanted to reduce his inventory to make room for new stock.†

A glance at the classified advertising in our local news-

* We bought some great *new* kitchenware at less than half price at one such sale. And a friend bid in enough paint to redo his entire house for about one-fourth the usual cost.

† This kind of auction always sounds promising, but frequently the stock has been diminished by being picked over in advance, so that not many of the choice items find their way to the auction block. If they do, they may go up with substantial reserves that equal—or even exceed—the previous retail price. If an occasional treasure does slip by, it will sometimes be bought by the auctioneer, or one of his colleagues, and the private buyer will have an opportunity to bid for it again at a later (and perhaps more elaborately conducted) auction. The mere fact that an item has been taken from the stock of an antiques shop seems sufficient to enhance its price at auction, where the words "This is *old!*" somehow serve to charm a forest of wildly waving hands from an otherwise quite sensible audience.

paper was sufficient to alert us to such sales. Then, after we had bought at one sale, we found that we received postcard announcements of future auctions. So one of the best ways to find an auction is to attend an auction. If the auctioneer runs a mailing list, you can ask to be added to it so that you will receive advance word of upcoming sales. Most auctioneers will be glad to do this, which again proves how important you are to the success of their business.

I know one auctioneer who charges $1 a year for his mimeographed mailings, but I know fifty who charge nothing. (One charges $100 for an annual subscription to his catalogues, which is something else entirely. The catalogues are worth the price, too!) Occasionally you will ask to be put on the mailing list of a particular gallery and not too graciously will be told that after you have established yourself as a regular customer through buying at three or four sales, your name will be considered for addition to the magic list. I suppose it is the auctioneer's responsibility to exercise a certain amount of selectivity in this respect. Printed materials—even postcards— do cost money. Addressograph plates have to be made and maintained. Clerical help is sometimes in short supply. Even at bulk rates, postage charges can be considerable. Probably the auctioneer who charges his customers $1 doesn't begin to break even on the cost of his mailings. But I didn't register for his list—largely because I felt that if I did it would be only fair of me to send $1 to each of the many auctioneers who manage, somehow, to absorb the cost of keeping me advised of their activities.* Plus which, the sales run by old $1-Fee-to-Receive-Our-Mailings were not all that special.

Anyway, almost before you know it, auction announcements

* If you find—as, for any number of reasons, you might—that you are no longer interested in receiving announcements from a particular auctioneer, it would be appropriate to send him a note to that effect, and to enclose the address from your most recent mailing. Provided, of course, the notices were being sent at his expense.

will begin to fill your mailbox. Your problem will quickly change from finding an auction to choosing which of several you will attend.

Probably you will select the first auction from your local newspaper. Look in the classified-advertising pages. Traditional auction days vary from town to town, and from auctioneer to auctioneer, but try Thursday's newspaper to find announcements of weekend sales. (The exhibition of a Saturday-morning sale might be held on Friday only, and you would not want to miss the opportunity for inspection.) If your newspaper publishes a Sunday edition, you will probably find the week's major auctions listed in it, although the descriptions will not always be complete.* The page or more of auction advertisements in the Sunday *New York Times* frequently includes important sales in Washington, D.C.; Chicago; Philadelphia; Boston and other cities, in addition to auctions, both great and small, being held in and around New York City.

In searching out auction news from your local paper, don't despair if you fail to find a separate department for auctions. Look under such related headings as MERCHANDISE OFFERINGS and BUSINESS OPPORTUNITIES. Look for auction ads in the entertainment pages, too. And on the "women's pages." Tucked in among the news of rummage sales and cake sales and bingo parties will be an occasional fund-raising auction held by a church or club.† Look under ORGANIZATIONS, or

---

* Don't ignore an auction simply because a newspaper advertisement does not mention a particular item in which you are interested. Space is limited. Late additions cannot be included. And some of the best auction finds are things that seemed not to be worth listing. Until you know the auctioneer, you can't evaluate a sale from a newspaper ad.

† Try them! They're often a lot of fun. Easy and relaxed. And sometimes you can make an astonishing buy. Most of the merchandise is donated. Much of it may be new. The auctioneer is usually contributing his services, or taking a small fee in lieu of his regular percentage. You are less likely to be "bid up" than at other auctions. And if one of the ladies has contributed a dusty treasure that she happened across while cleaning out the attic, you just might make a worthwhile find, especially since the lots probably have not been too carefully appraised.

THIS WEEK IN . . . or wherever else such local activities are listed.

Try your classified telephone book, too. I am always surprised when friends ask us how we discover all the different auctions we attend, as if we had developed some secret system for rooting out sales. Actually the very phrase "Public Auction" sets forth the fundamental lack of secrecy that is essential to the success of an auction. But newspaper advertising of other than classified size can take a big bite out of an auctioneer's commissions, which is one reason some auctioneers will accumulate many hundreds of lots for a combined sale that might last three or more days in order to increase the potential return on their advertising expense. And not every auctioneer will invest in even a tiny ad for every sale he holds. Not that he wouldn't like to. He knows that the more people he can attract to the auction, the better the prices will be. But if increasing his audience involves renting a larger hall, putting extra workers on his crew and spending more money on advertising, he might have to forgo those extras in the interest of operating on a financially sound basis. Nevertheless, even the most pared-down auction establishment is going to have a telephone.

Look under AUCTIONEERS in your classified telephone directory. Surprised to see how many there are? Practically on your doorstep! And out of that listing, it might be that only two or three names will be familiar from the auction advertisements in the newspapers. What are all the other auctioneers doing? Well, some of them undoubtedly specialize in the sale of things you and I are probably never going to buy in auction lots. (Heavy machinery. Pharmacy supplies. Livestock. Farm produce.) Others will be part-timers who conduct occasional

---

Additionally, these sales give you a good chance to perfect your auction technique —like an apprentice chef learning to pipe decorations in mashed potato before graduating to fancy meringues and frostings.

auctions as a sideline. One or two will be technically in retirement, doing maybe one sale a year—as a favor to a friend, or because they can't quite bring themselves to quit the scene completely. Among the others, you are likely to discover auctioneers who will be glad to send you notices of forthcoming sales, many of which might happen to be held in neighboring towns. It is not unheard of for an auctioneer to have most of his contacts in an area other than the town in which he maintains his residence or office. You could, of course, find out about these sales by subscribing to *all* the local newspapers published within a hundred-mile area. But a few calls or letters to the auctioneers in your classified telephone directory will save you a lot of money and effort. If the AUCTIONEERS listing should seem disappointing, you might check related listings such as APPRAISERS; ART GALLERIES; FURNITURE, USED; BOOKS, USED AND RARE. Make a few calls. Even if those dealers do not hold auctions, they are apt to know the men who do.

The classified-directory technique is a good one to use when traveling, too. On the road, we will usually buy a small-town newspaper plus whatever city paper also serves the area. If neither happens to yield an intriguing auction, we look up AUCTIONEERS in the telephone directory and start making calls. We have found a lot of good sales that way.

Another reliable technique for finding an auction is to ask someone else *at* an auction. This presumes, of course, that you have, through either the newspapers or your telephone campaign, located auction number one. When the sale is finished —perhaps while you are waiting in line to settle your bill, or to claim your purchases—talk to one or two of your neighbors. The spirit of competition that would advise against such an approach during the sale will have been dispelled by the final fall of the auctioneer's hammer. If you can remember any of the lots that your neighbor bid in, tell him that you think he certainly did well for himself that day. Immediately, you have suggested that you think he is a clever and experienced auction buyer. Usually you will be told about other, more important purchases he has made at other sales. Auction buffs discuss auctions the way balletomanes compare *Giselles*; you will easily be able to steer the conversation toward other sales that your new acquaintance attends, and without too much prodding, he will reveal where and how they are held and what you could expect to find there.* In addition to finding new auctions to attend, you also will pick up clues about which auctions you can best afford to avoid.

All of which you should, of course, take with the proverbial grain of salt. There are auctioneers of whom I have heard discouraging reports, yet from whom I have made some of our best purchases. There are others with whom my experience has been negative, although friends have bought with impressive success at their sales. Personalities are a not insignificant element at an auction. Maybe it's just a matter of what the writers of modern romance novels used to refer to as "chemistry." An auctioneer will have his prejudices, you know, and like most prejudices, his are apt to be thoroughly irrational. Maybe he just can't stand people in red sweaters, or corduroy vests, or fur hats. Or, more probably, the auctioneer fails to take someone's bids because he simply cannot see them. Most

---

* In time, this will happen to you too. It is practically standard procedure. If it sounds like a capsule version of *All About Eve*, bear in mind that it does have the advantage of spreading the word on any flagrantly dishonest operators. "I wouldn't go to one of *his* sales! He's such a fraud! Runs you up to the sky and then bids everything in for himself! You see the same things at every one of his auctions!" That kind of between-bidders gossip can soon leave a crooked auctioneer facing an empty salesroom, or send him in search of suckers in another town. There are uncountable legal loopholes through which an unethical auctioneer can smoothly slip. And the very gift of gab, the manner of genial, or dynamic, authority that is essential to his success on the platform, is a powerful weapon against the complaints of a dissatisfied customer. Such an operator, however, is apt to have a hard time of it once the word on him starts being passed from one auction addict to another.

auctioneers will try to seat as large an audience as possible at a sale. But maximum seating frequently results in some fairly undesirable locations, and an unacknowledged bidder may be sitting in a blind spot. (*See Chapter 4: How to Attend an Auction.*) Occupying a better seat at the same sale, you might have only praise for the auctioneer's fairness and skill, while your less-well-situated competitor, bidding unseen throughout the session, might well condemn the man as anything from myopic to crooked.

This is as bad a place as any to consider the subject of dishonest auctioneers. And let's face it, some of them are. So are some automobile mechanics, some lawyers, some insurance agents, some politicians, some pharmacists, some literary agents, some bartenders, some grocers, some . . . well, if there's a dollar to be made at it, it is always possible that someone a little unethical will be in there trying to squeeze out a dollar and a half. And if you find that your grocer is cheating you, or that his cashier is overringing, what do you do? You continue to shop for groceries, but you buy at a different store. After all, there are honest grocers, even as there are honest auctioneers. All things being equal, however, the dishonest auctioneer has at his disposal a catalogue of devices that would make the most corrupt politician look to his laurels.

I find it hard to tell whether or not an auctioneer is operating honestly the first time I attend one of his sales. For one thing, the excitement of going to a new auction makes objectivity difficult. And it may take a bit of acquaintance to become thoroughly comfortable with an auctioneer's style. Then too, most—perhaps all—of the audience will be unknown and, accordingly, impossible to predict. Still, there are a few things to watch for, since they *might* indicate that the auction is being conducted along somewhat irregular lines.

(1) The auctioneer's descriptions obviously exaggerate the worth or character of a lot. (Of course, he could simply be

mistaken. Or you might be. So give him the benefit of the doubt, unless he makes it patently obvious that he does not deserve it.)

(2) An outrageously high opening bid is requested and either: (a) is instantly received, but not supported by subsequent bidding; (b) fails, at which point the bidding is opened at a ridiculously lower figure, the lot closing at a bid far below that which was asked to open. (The first is probably a fake bid, although it could represent an individual caprice. The second does happen from time to time at a perfectly legitimate sale, although most auctioneers would refuse to open at a decidedly unfavorable bid and, if the lot has not been greatly misrepresented, probably would not need to.)

(3) Many lots are passed. (Again, an honest auctioneer sometimes will, for various reasons, remove an unsold lot from the block. For example, he might feel that he cannot expect to reach a consignor's reserve. The key word is "many." An experienced auctioneer will not accept consignments on which impossible reserves have been established. He might miscalculate on one or two lots in the course of a sale. But with the possible exception of pawnbrokers' auctions, at which reserve figures might be based on unredeemed pledges, if lot after lot is passed unsold, the auctioneer may be offering you his personal merchandise, or inventory borrowed from a retail shop, to be sold at retail—or better—prices.)

(4) The auctioneer announces the name, number or initials of the successful bidder on some lots, but fails to identify the buyers of others. (There is less reason for suspicion when *no* identifications are given throughout the sale. Some reputable auction rooms consistently work that way. Others are equally consistent in declaring the winner of every lot. But when the names of the buyers of some lots are clearly enunciated, while others are unintelligibly mumbled—usually as an accompaniment to the scribbling of elaborate marginal notes on the

auctioneer's sheet—it would not be unreasonable to think that at least some of those bids were tendered by phantoms. On the other hand, when an auctioneer, with obvious emphasis, announces the identity of every successful order bidder, I am inclined to be more suspicious than when he simply says, "Sold to the order." Custom varies, of course, but identifying by name—and sometimes by address! "Dr. Soandso of Brooklyn," for instance—the winner of a lot sold on an advance bid frequently is done to convince the audience that a nonexistent order bid was legitimate.)

(5) An exceptional number and variety of lots are won by a single bidder. ("Shill" is a word that falls unpleasantly on the ear of any auctioneer. Most of them will deny the shill's existence, though many are those who have made his acquaintance. Ask an auctioneer his opinion of shills and you will think you had just asked Dracula to admire the fine carving on a crucifix. Some auctioneers will swear that they never employ shills. Others privately admit that they occasionally fall back on them. "But only rarely . . . to get the bidding under way . . . or for the protection of one of our consignors." Some shills are brazenly easy to identify. Others are so skillful that they blend invisibly into the bidding pattern of the audience—and may, indeed, be legitimately buying certain lots while bidding others in for the house. That one buyer happens to be winning a preponderance of lots at a particular sale should not irrefutably identify him as a shill. Everyone has an occasional "big day," and oddly enough, the more items one wins, the more he is inclined to continue bidding and buying. The auctioneer knows this and uses it to his advantage by giving the generous buyer a quick knock or two in the course of the sale. This impulsive gesture, however, is occasionally used to make it easier for the auctioneer to bid up the thus-reassured big spender, who, beaming expansively, is likely to overbid on following lots. There are

people who, in the course of a single sale, will bid on anything from a toothpick holder to a tabernacle mirror to a tortoise-shell comb to an elegant trumeau to three old tractor seats. Again, if you see someone buying with such catholicity of interest, do not immediately assume that he is a shill. Watch, if you can, to see if he meticulously records his various purchases as they are knocked down to him. A legitimate buyer usually does this. At best, most shills are haphazard about it. Some don't even make a pretense of noting their purchases, which makes them almost pathetically easy to spot.)

(6) Many lots are introduced with advance bids, which the auctioneer announces as the amount for an opening bid, inviting an increase thereon. (Technically, this is unfair to the advance bidder, if there actually was one. *See Chapter 4: How to Attend an Auction.* The purpose of an order bid is to establish a maximum offer the absent bidder does not wish to exceed, rather than a minimum start without which the sale of the lot cannot proceed. Most auctioneers realize that it is to their advantage to stimulate bidding from the audience and, consequently, will open a lot several bids under the advance figure.)

(7) As an adjunct to auction sales, the management operates an antiques shop, second-hand-furniture store, interior-decorating service, carpet shop, clock shop, art gallery, or similarly related establishment that could serve as an outlet for unsold items and, conversely, as a source of potential auction lots that might be drawn from inventory. (Nothing basically dishonest about that, except when what was announced as a public auction is run as an elaborately staged private sale.)

(8) An "estate" handily consists of one of everything: one stein, one moustache cup, one shaving mug, one lamp, one table, one practically complete set of china, one chimney-garniture set, one fire screen, one mirror, one footstool . . . and on, and on, and on, as if for generations the family had

meticulously accumulated and saved only unique items. (Think how different your "estate" would look if it were lotted up for sale at auction. So, undoubtedly, would any genuine estate. The one-of-each assemblage has probably been carefully composed with the aid of a wholesaler or importer, to whom the auctioneer will return any items that fail to reach an agreed-upon price.)

(9) A "collection" consists of fairly routine items of uniformly mediocre quality. (Not every collector is a connoisseur, certainly, but somewhere along the way, something truly superlative—or utterly worthless—is almost certain to find its way into any genuine collection. If the "collection" is all of a piece, the chances are good that it was collected by the auctioneer directly in the importer's storeroom. Again with certain specific price restrictions below which it will not be sold.)

(10) A house sale includes many obvious additions. (Oriental rugs that do not fit the rooms in which they are shown, and seem not only the wrong size, but far too luxurious for the home in which they are displayed. Paintings that are not consistent with the taste shown in other furnishings. Furniture that looks too large or too small in relation to the rooms. Lamps, bronzes, ivories, silver, crystal and bric-a-brac that do not seem "at home" in the general decor. Some auctioneers make a specialty of selling off the contents of houses, provided they are allowed to lot in some of their own merchandise. Invariably, the additions are the most attractive lots in the sale, but they are seldom bought through open competitive bidding. Most often they will be bought back by the auctioneer and moved on to the next sale.)

If the auction that you have found sounds some of these warning signals: don't panic. Nothing very terrible is going to happen to you. Some of the most corrupt auctioneers are the most entertaining. Their extravagant descriptions are far more enjoyable than the staid, succinct lot announcements that are characteristic of some of the more reputable auctions. You might even be able to make a few buys, provided you can convince the auctioneer that you will not be bid up. (*See Chapter 6: How to Avoid Bidding Against Yourself.*) If this sounds terribly contradictory, remember that even a dishonest auctioneer must make a few actual sales if only to cover his expenses. He may not begin giving things away, but if many items have been passed, or bought back, he might have to knock down a few lots in order to come away from the auction in the black.

Which is why it is best not to be discouraged by the negative comments you may hear when you ask someone where to find an auction. Go and see for yourself. But keep your eyes open!

Antiques dealers will frequently put down auction sales, encouraging you to buy instead from a reputable shop—such, no doubt, as theirs. After they have shared their favorite auction horror stories with you, they can usually be depended upon to know about any sales in their area. And if you attend the sale, you might be amused to find yourself bidding alongside your cautionary informant.

If you are traveling and the newspapers are sold out, the page in question is missing from your classified telephone directory, the antiques shops are closed, and you still haven't succeeded in locating an auction, then broaden your field of inquiry. It's more fun to go to an auction than to sit in your room and watch television, isn't it? (Or will be, until some genius gets around to presenting a weekly auction on TV.) See if you can rouse someone at the Chamber of Commerce. Call the local Rotary; it might be a bit out of line, but they are usually up on local events. Ask at restaurants. (We found out about one of our favorite auctions from a waitress who, after an uncertain start, managed with the help of her colleagues to send us off on one of those back-road junkets that are an auction addict's dream.) Ask at the gasoline stations, too. Motel managers somehow never seem to know about events not being held on their premises, but the maid who cleans your room frequently does. Auctions are currently very big with the under-thirty crowd, so cast your questions accordingly. Bear in mind that if someone tells you, "They used to have sales every week up at the . . . ," the chances are excellent that auctions are still being held there. Certainly it will be worth your time to drive to wherever-it-was to find out. You may discover, as we once did, that you have arrived at a livestock auction barn. On the other hand, it is entirely possible that you will have found an exciting new auction to attend —in which case, your next move is the all-imporant inspection.

3 HOW TO INSPECT AN AUCTION

In a sense, attending the exhibition, which is also known as the preview, or inspection, is more important than being present at the sales session. It is possible to purchase lots at auction without actually attending the sale, but it is a very good rule to bid on no item that you have not previously had an opportunity to inspect. You should consider the exhibition an essential part of the auction, and an element of the sale that is not to be neglected. We will frequently bypass an auction that we have not had an opportunity to inspect, even though we could comfortably arrive in time for the sale. If we do yield to temptation and find ourselves sitting before a series of lots that we haven't had a chance to view in advance, we try to regard the auction as purely educational and recreational, and do our best to keep out of the bidding.

You will find that you can have a very good time at an auction even if you never make a bid. On the other hand, there's nothing like an overpriced lemon to spoil an otherwise perfect evening. Auction fever is contagious, and once the bidding is under way it is difficult for good sense to prevail with reminders that one is bidding blindly on an item that, however attractive it might look from the deceptively close range of a front-row seat, might prove disappointing under the intimate circumstances of ownership. (I know, because I have a perfectly useless piece of velvet-edged painted burlap that, even up close, looks convincingly like a fine old tapestry. Imagine how terrific it looked draped over the auction block! I had visions of willing it eventually to the Metropolitan Museum. I had one brief moment of glory when the hanging was knocked down to me for $50. I had another moment—not quite so splendid—when my treasure was delivered to me and my mistake was unveiled along with my extravagance. Had I inspected that auction, I would have recognized the "tapestry" for what it was: an extremely well-executed fake, carefully disguised with a border of extremely well-faked "antique" velvet. A true tapestry, incidentally, is the same on both sides. There may be threads and knots and an uneven surface to the reverse, but the design will be identical on either face. If it isn't, then whatever else it may be, the fabric on which you are bidding is not a genuine tapestry, and you will want to adjust your bid accordingly or, more probably, not bid at all. My $50 length of burlap was purchased early in my auction-going youth, or I would have known how unlikely it was to acquire an item for 5 percent of its value. (*See Chapter 5: How to Make a Killing.*)

A good rule to follow if you don't want to get hurt when buying at auction—and by hurt, I mean both emotional and financial disappointment—is *never* to bid for any item that you have not first inspected. If you haven't seen it at the time of the exhibition, skip it at the time of sale.

"Please examine your choice carefully before bidding—everything is sold *as is*, in accordance with printed catalogue descriptions and the 'Conditions of Sale.' Read descriptions carefully when examining the objects," Parke-Bernet Galleries recommends in its printed "Tips for New Bidders." Without exception, auctioneers agree. "Inspection is vital," insists Hy Fogel, director of Long Island's Nassau Gallery. After more than twenty years as an auctioneer, Fogel maintains that "No one should purchase anything at auction unless he has seen it at the exhibition. He should examine it closely. Handle it. Inspect it as to color, and other indications of authenticity. And determine if it is in proper or 'as is' condition. He should thoroughly familiarize himself with the piece, and if he has questions about it, he should discuss them with the auctioneer." Prominently displayed in Hy Fogel's auction room is this message: NASSAU GALLERY LTD. FIRMLY STATES THAT YOU, THE AUCTION BUYER, SHOULD ATTEND THE EXHIBITION BEFORE YOU BUY. THE SMART BUYER USUALLY DOES.

Of course, you are going to break this rule—all of us do, and not always with unpleasant results, which is one reason the rule is so difficult to follow. When you do make an exception, try to keep your wits about you and hold your bids within reason. Remember that you are buying blindly, so make your bids appropriate to the grab-bag nature of a blind item. Don't be too impressed by the fact that someone else seems to think the item up for sale is worth a high bid. The rival bidder may be a plant. Or he might be bidding blindly, even as you are. Of course, he also might be an expert who has the advantage of having attended the exhibition. In that case, he's in a much better position to evaluate the lot in question.

No matter whether your rival is a plant, another blind bidder or an expert, you will do well to retire before the bids get too high. Console yourself with the promise that you will devote more attention to the exhibition before the next auction. For one thing, you can't possibly compete if you are bidding blindly against an informed expert. Or the lot may be defective in some way that your competitor failed to notice— in which case, *his* carelessness is going to cost *you* money. And you wouldn't want to be run up by a shill, or by another blind bidder. Bid, if you must, on occasional items that escaped your notice at the time of exhibition, but limit your bids to amounts that you can afford to lose. And be prepared for more disappointments than delights. Acquiring three or four chipped, cracked, mended, incomplete, wobbly, nonworking, expensive-to-repair or otherwise useless items will go far to impress you with the importance of bidding only on those lots you have carefully examined.

The only way for those of us not gifted with X-ray vision and 100-percent clairvoyance to tell treasure from trash is to attend the exhibition. If you have ever watched an expert appraise an article, you've no doubt been impressed by the thoroughness with which he examines the piece. And remember, he's applying years of training and experience. It stands to reason, then, doesn't it, that if an appraiser needs time and close concentration to evaluate an item, you and I, lacking that special expertise, ought to need at least a few minutes to consider the lots that interest us at an auction preview?

There is much to be said—particularly in regard to antique furniture—for the simple and instant evaluation based on nothing more than the look of quality. Good pieces *look* good. You can quite literally believe your eyes, once you learn to recognize that look. The best way to make its acquaintance is to do a little homework, browsing in the better shops, galleries and museums. Attending auction exhibitions has the added advantage of giving you an opportunity to inspect these treasures at close range instead of from behind velvet ropes. Generally, you can also carefully handle the pieces in which you are interested. And you should! The look of quality can help you recognize an important piece, but you will need to get much closer to determine whether or not the item has been repaired. And whether or not the repairs have been properly done. And whether the item is completely original or a cannibalized piece, or if it still wears its proper brasses, or if the hinges have been replaced, or, or, or . . . In short, you can trust that wonderful look of quality sufficiently to let it lead you to a piece that is worth the time and trouble of a closer and more detailed inspection.

Careful examination is even more important in regard to smaller items, even if the financial penalty might be lower—and in many cases it is not, especially if one is considering the finest porcelains or art glass—since the opportunities for disappointment are greater. You will want to use those goblets, or that decanter, or the tureen, or the sugar basin, or the cut-glass fruit bowl, and chips, cracks, nicks and other imperfections are best taken note of in advance, and your bids scaled accordingly.

"Age, condition and style all affect the price of an auction offering," says Timothy C. Tetlow, manager of Parke-Bernet's PB-84 division, "but use is also a very important consideration. Of course the article should look attractive, but it should serve the purpose for which it is purchased. Sales at PB-84 appeal to the public at large. People come here to buy for utilitarian reasons and for decorative reasons, whereas at the main gallery [Parke-Bernet] they might be more interested in the value something offers as an investment."

The auctioneer will describe the lot when it is put up for sale, but the description is apt to be rather general, and it is well to remember that even the most meticulously honest auctioneer is interested primarily in realizing the highest possible price for every lot offered and can, perhaps, be forgiven if he fails to point out a tiny chip, a minor crack or even a blatantly bad repair. Actually, he is not obliged to mention any defect. Many auctioneers do not. Most will preface their sale sessions with an announcement to the effect that all items are sold "as is," and that while every attempt is made to have descriptions of articles accurately reflect the true character and condition of the item, the terms of sale relieve the vender of any responsibility for authenticity. As usual, there are exceptions. Included in the printed "Conditions of Sale" of Parke-Bernet Galleries is the following:

1. All property is sold "as is" and neither the Galleries nor its Consignor makes any warranties or representations of any kind or nature with respect to the property, and in no event shall they be responsible for the correctness, nor deemed to have made any representation or warranty, of description, genuineness, authorship, attribution, provenience, period, culture, source, origin or condition of the property and no statement in the catalogue or made at the sale or in the bill of sale or invoice or elsewhere shall be deemed such a warranty or representation or an assumption of liability.

2. Notwithstanding the preceding condition, if within twenty-one (21) days of the sale of any lot, the purchaser gives notice in writing to the Galleries that the lot so sold is a forgery and, if within fourteen (14) days after such notice the purchaser returns the lot to the Galleries in the same condition as when sold, and proves beyond reasonable doubt that the returned lot is in fact a forgery and that this was not indicated by a fair reading of the catalogue, the Galleries as agent for the Consignor will rescind the sale and refund the purchase price received by them.

Undoubtedly there are other galleries with similar provisions set forth in their conditions of sale. In one form or another, something comparable to Paragraph 1 can be found in the terms of sale at almost any auction in the United States. You might have to cross the Atlantic to duplicate the provisions of Paragraph 2. If you have only to cross the street to accomplish this, take a bow, and realize how lucky you are.

If an auctioneer presents a lot as sterling silver and you find it to be only silverplate, you will usually be able to return your overpriced purchase; the same is generally true of items described as "signed" that turn out either to be unsigned or to bear some signature other than that which was promised. I have found few auctioneers deliberately misrepresenting items. Those who do, by the way, are so outrageous that their descriptions are almost ludicrous, if not enraging. (Anyone who doesn't know Woolworth glass from Waterford crystal can make some pretty fantastic purchases at auctions run by those boys, most of whom are given to describing every item as "very old, very rare," a phrase that does seem to help them move the bidding along, since the average buyer of antiques seems to feel that "old" is synonymous with "desirable."*) On the other hand, there are very few auctioneers who will go out of their way to tell you about minor flaws or imperfections. If you find one who does—consistently—put away the lantern, for you have indeed discovered an honest man. In fairness to the others—and they include the proprietors of some of the most celebrated galleries—let us say that they perhaps have failed to note the minor, or sometimes the major, flaws. They may handle two or three hundred articles in the course of a sale. Certain imperfections may indeed pass unnoticed. Which is all the more reason why it is important for you to make a special point of attending the exhibition.

There are three auctioneers whom I have found consistently good about pointing out damaged items. Even at their auctions, I like to be sure that I have carefully inspected any lots on which I am interested in bidding. For one thing, a tiny chip on the inside of a teapot might be sufficient to cause the auctioneer to describe the item as "imperfect," although it might in no way diminish my interest in the article if I plan to use it only as a cabinet piece. Of course, I will bid less for it. But if I were guided solely by the auctioneer's description, I might be discouraged from bidding at all. On the other hand, this same careful auctioneer might accurately announce that the only flaw in an elaborately veneered table is that a

---

* You and I know that all the grime in the world can't hide the fire of fine Waterford, just as we know—because we *touched* it during the exhibition—the sharp, clean edges and heavy weight that distinguish a piece of cut glass from its poor, blunt but often brilliant pressed imitation. But if we hadn't given those pieces our attention when we inspected the lots, we might have been taken in by that "very old, very rare" gambit.

tiny piece or two of the exquisite pictorial marquetry is missing. This might not sound like a particularly important defect, but a quick glance during the exhibition would have revealed that it called for a delicate bit of repair work that could be undertaken only by a skilled artisan who would have to carefully match woods and finishes to make the replacement pieces blend unnoticeably into the intricate pattern of the original work. Again, the auctioneer's description, however accurate, completely failed to convey the kind of information that could have been developed in a few minutes at the time of inspection.

So let it be agreed, if we plan to attend the auction, we will also plan to attend the exhibition. We will consider the preview an important aspect of the auction sale. We can, if we wish, place order bids on items that we have inspected, but we will not—except on rare and carefully considered occasions —make bids at auction on items that we have not seen on exhibition. Most auctioneers will accept advance bids on lots in which you are interested. I think it might be going a bit too far to ask for the privilege on many, low-cost items, but there are some patient gentlemen who will agree to accommodate you. If you know that you will be unable to attend an auction at which there are one or two important lots that you would like to purchase, and you have bought from the auctioneer previously and found him to be reliable, ask him to execute an order bid for you. You can do that when you attend the exhibition or by mail, telegram or telephone—often right up to the moment bidding for the lot in question is closed. You also can increase your offer, or withdraw it. If you decide that you wish to reduce it, however, your instructions should be confirmed before the start of the sale session. But you are in no position to exercise any of these options if you have not attended the exhibition.

Auction announcements usually detail the dates and hours

of exhibition. If you find one that does not, or if you are unfamiliar with the policy of a particular auctioneer, don't hesitate to telephone to find out when the lots will be available for inspection. Most auctioneers want you to take advantage of the hours of exhibition, but very few of them will welcome you at times other than those set aside for that purpose. An auction room is a busy place. There is much moving about of large, clumsy, valuable and often breakable merchandise. If you are on the premises when new consignments are being brought in, you are not only going to be in the way, you are apt to be in danger. In addition to being a safety hazard, you are also a potential nuisance. If the proprietor is busy directing the moving of furniture, or setting up chairs, or ticketing lots in sequence of sale, he simply does not have the time or inclination to answer your questions, hand down shelf items, or show pieces from closed-cabinet displays. Therefore, for your safety and convenience, and for the auctioneer's peace of mind, let the time of your visit coincide with the regular hours of exhibition. These may vary from one or two hours immediately before a sale, to day-long inspections for a full week or two prior to a major auction. Don't think that by crashing the exhibition before the time scheduled, you will enjoy a private preview. For one thing, certain lots in which you might be interested may not yet have been set up for display. And the catalogues might not yet be available. Or all the lots numbered.*

* Of course, if the auctioneer happens to invite you to come in for an early look at something in which he thinks you will be interested, that is another matter entirely. Even so, it is a good idea to make a specific appointment. And don't get so involved in conversation that your inspection is less than usually thorough. If you find the lot defective in some way, there is nothing wrong with pointing that out, but don't expect to save money by unfairly deprecating the piece—or by waxing enthusiastic. If the auctioneer knew enough to call you in reference to whatever, you can be confident that he knows his customer and his merchandise quite well indeed. Much as he might appreciate the benefit of any

If possible, plan to attend the exhibition at least a day in advance of the sale session. This will give you an opportunity to prepare a list of items on which you want to place bids, and to establish your personal price ceiling to be used as a bidding limit on each lot in which you are interested. It will also allow you time to check catalogues and reference books and to make a quick trip to a nearby shop or museum in the event you want to do a bit of fast authenticating. It will give you a chance to look up markings, signatures, hallmarks and dates and—in the case of new or secondhand merchandise—to check advertisements or local stores for current prices on comparable items.

One of the best ways to set a ceiling price for an item is to imagine it on display in the window of a retail shop. See a price indicated on it. Go ahead. Picture the price clearly marked in dollars and cents. On the windshield of a car. On a tag dangling from one arm of a chandelier. In black wax numbers on the rim of a plate. Now—how much does it say? How much? Keep trying, if you can't immediately visualize it. What you want to determine is at what price you would feel impelled to rush into the shop to buy it. Unless you have been totally unrealistic, *that* would be a satisfactory limit to set on your bid.

You should expect to save a minimum of 20 to 40 percent of the established retail price on any item purchased at auction. Often, of course, you will save 50 percent or more. And the potential saving on antiques is limited only by your ingenuity, the expertise of the auctioneer and the competence, or lack of competence, of competitive bidders. There is about as much point in paying more than the going retail price for

---

special information developed by your inspection, he is not going to be impressed if you suggest that you might give $50 for something each of you knows to be worth $500.

an item bought at auction as there is in paying the same amount for dinner at a cafeteria and in a three-star restaurant. And yet I once saw a woman buy a three-tray plush-lined jewel box for twice the price at which the identical item was being sold at a department store less than two blocks from the auction room. And if the lock or the hinges happened to be broken on the box bought at the department store, the uninformed bidder would have had no trouble in returning the item—a privilege she paid double *not* to enjoy. Enthusiasm and the spirit of competition can spur you on to recklessness unless you take advantage of the opportunity to inspect the auction lots before they are put up for bids, and to do a bit of comparison shopping before you establish your bidding maximums.

If you are interested in jewelry, or paintings and sculpture, and do not feel competent to evaluate the items offered, the extra time between your inspection and the sale session will give you an opportunity to revisit the exhibition in the company of an expert. *Hire* someone. If he is worth listening to, he will expect to be paid for his time, and the fee, which you will have established in advance, will pay substantial dividends in terms of the confidence with which you will then attend the auction. Don't rely on the opinions of "well-informed" friends. You will understand why not the first time a "friend" you have asked to accompany you to an exhibition turns up bidding against you at the sale. There are no friends at auction. Anyone who argues differently has something left to learn.

Making your inspection at least a day in advance of the sale will also give you a chance to imagine your planned purchases situated in your home. To check whether or not that 97-inch cabinet will clear your dining-room ceiling. And if it will, whether or not you will be able to sit at the dining table once the cabinet stands behind it. After all, if you not only can't use it but have to leave it lying on its side in the entrance hall, your auction bargain can quickly become a cumbersome and costly frustration.

Along with an open mind, a curious nose and an eagerness for adventure, take a stenographer's notebook to the exhibition. An ordinary stenographer's pad, with a spiral binding at the top and two cardboard flaps that form an acceptable support when you want to write on the double-columned pages, is the most helpful piece of auction equipment that I have found. You can cram a year's auction notations into one of these pads, and you will undoubtedly be glad to have those notes to refer to—especially if a time comes when you are ready to sell one of your treasures and you want to determine a respectable price. Don't delude yourself into believing you will remember the exact amount you spent for every piece that you buy. You won't. Take my word for it. Keeping your auction notes on file will settle many an argument, and provide a permanent record not only of what you paid for the items that you won, but also of what items were offered at which sale, what your estimated bid was and—provided you take the trouble to jot it down—what the lot sold for.

At most of the larger auction sales, you will find special catalogues. These may range from a simple mimeographed list to an elaborate, expensively printed illustrated booklet that, if it represents an important sale, may often serve as an important reference source for historians, museums, appraisers and collectors. You will certainly want to purchase a catalogue of the sale, and the time to purchase it is at the exhibition. But even with your catalogue at hand—and there are several reasons (some of which I'll go into later) why you might not have one at hand—you will still want to have your steno pad with you at the exhibition and also at the sale.

For one thing, many auction lists are just that: lists. Single-spaced mimeographed pages, poorly reproduced and, perhaps, stapled together at the top. You will find them highly unsatisfactory for the kind of meaningful notations that you want to make when inspecting an auction. On an auction list, you might circle the lot numbers of items that you are interested in buying, but you will usually find it a little crowded when you're ready to write in your maximum bids, and that's an important part of the information you will want to have at your fingertips once the sale gets under way. You also might find that your indicated bids get confused with the prices on other lots, that your various comments tend to run together and that two or more similar items listed together are pretty hard to untangle in the heat of competitive bidding. By all means, try to obtain a catalogue if one has been prepared for the sale, but take your notebook to the exhibition and to the auction.

There are, of course, many auctions for which no catalogue is prepared. At these sales, your steno pad is essential. Don't expect to get by with any little sheet of paper, or a couple of pages stolen from your address book. It is really exasperating to try to find a specific note when you've carelessly recorded your impressions of the exhibition. Once the auction begins, you are going to want to concentrate on the bidding and not on a search for random pages on which you have scribbled a few already meaningless numbers.

Catalogues are sometimes in short supply. If you go to the exhibition during its last hours (and that is not necessarily a bad time to go, by the way, since lots are sometimes added or withdrawn right up to the final moments before the sale, and you will have a chance to consider last-minute changes), there may be no more catalogues available. On the other hand, if you attend the opening session of the auction preview (and that has its advantages too, since it will give you more time to consider the items on which you plan to bid, and to carefully estimate the extent of your interest), you may find that the catalogues have not yet arrived.*

Devote a separate line in your notebook to each item that interests you. Jot down the lot number first. Then a general description of the article. If there is more than one piece in the lot, you'll have room to note whether it is a pair or a set or an assortment and how many pieces are included. The auction tag will usually have "pr." or the number of pieces listed just below or opposite the auction lot number. Thus "#857/pr." would indicate a matched pair of chairs, candlesticks, vases, figurines, or whatever, while "#857/2" *might* mean that the lot includes a matched pair of items, but could mean that it consists of two separate items that are totally unrelated. A mark reading "#857/8" indicates that lot No. 857 consists of eight pieces and you will do well to look for seven other articles marked 857, or for seven nearby items that are unmarked and obviously included with the numbered piece. If there is any doubt about the contents of a mixed lot, ask the auctioneer or the clerk to show you the contents of lot No. 857, and be sure to jot down the number of pieces and

---

*In line with what are, admittedly, contradictory recommendations, bear in mind that there are advantages to both early and late inspection. Ideally, a thorough inspection of the exhibition would be made at the earliest possible session, and a final, last-minute check for new additions, withdrawals, lot changes or possible damage to previously inspected lots (it does happen!) made just before the start of the sale. If that seems like an awful lot of inspecting, then settle, whenever possible, for the earlier session. You can take some comfort from the knowledge that important pieces are seldom among the last-minute additions to a sale. Most often the auctioneer will want to hold a major item until a later sale at which it can receive the attention (and advertising) it deserves. He might leave it prominently displayed in the gallery, as a kind of preview of coming attractions. It stands to reason, then, doesn't it, that he'd be foolish to waste an important lot by adding it to a sale at the last minute? And auctioneers don't stay in business by being foolish.

description of each so that there won't be any confusion when you want to bid, or when you are ready to claim your purchases. The time to find out is at the exhibition.

After the general description, you'll want to put down any pertinent comments on the condition of the piece. Damaged, repaired, chipped, one foot missing, knobs replaced—even "Matches Susie's vanity set"—will help you recall the item when you sit down to prepare your auction list and estimate a reasonable bid.

Take along a decent and dependable pen, too. I find that a ball-point pen with a pocket clip on it is best. For one thing, when you want two hands free to lift down an item from a shelf, you can clip your pen onto the spiral of your steno pad. If you value the linings of jackets, the survival of pockets and the contents of your handbag, choose a pen with a retractable point. Don't rely on a pencil. Pencils are less than satisfactory for purposes of the auction inspection, or when you attend the sale. For one thing, pencil points wear down quickly, and pencil sharpeners are not standard equipment in auction rooms. For another, pencil notes smudge and fade, and the whole point of your exhibition notes is to have them crisp and legible at the time of sale. You could, of course, carry five or ten good, well-pointed hard-lead pencils with you, or a mechanical pencil, but one trusty ball-point pen is much easier to manage. Many auction rooms will provide you with pencils. Often they may be sufficiently hard and efficiently sharpened. Equally often—in fact, *always*, to judge by my experience— they are uniformly three inches or less in length. This makes writing with them for any reasonable length of time something less than a joyous experience. Your notes will be easier to read, unsmudged and permanent, and you will run less risk of writer's cramp, if you take the trouble to carry along a good reliable pen when you go to inspect an auction. Tuck a spare one in your pocket or purse in case, in the course of a long day's inspection, it doesn't turn out to be as reliable a pen as you anticipated.

You will want to take a small magnet with you also. Nothing very elaborate—a toy magnet from the dime store will do. You'll find it invaluable when it comes to testing the authenticity of bronzes. Bronzes are not magnetic. Fake bronzes are likely to be made with iron. Your toy magnet can help you avoid buying a piece of gilded iron at a bronze price. Sometimes the magnet will tell you more than the auctioneer or the catalogue about the character of a "bronze" piece. There also may be times when your magnet will help you identify a valuable Oriental bronze that the rest of the crowd might pass by, thinking it nothing but an old iron pot or a cuspidor.

A small magnifying glass will also come in handy at the inspection. Some dealers make a big point of always carrying a jeweler's loupe (specifically necessary only for an expert examination of precious stones, such as diamonds) or a linen tester wherever they go, but magnifying glasses are easier to use and will almost always answer your exhibition needs. Hallmarked silver is easy to identify, provided you can identify the hallmarks. Squint all you want: years and many polishings (and occasional counterfeits) can go far toward making those identifications illegible. A pocket magnifying glass can go a long way toward bringing them to light. (It can also help you see whether the marks have been, perhaps, lifted from one piece and soldered into another in the interest of grafting on a bit of history and some extra value. Breathe on the hallmark. The condensed moisture of your breath will bring out the outlines of the bit of inlaid silver. The magnifying glass will enlarge them into shining barriers.) The glass has hundreds of uses at the inspection. It will help make the tiniest, most spidery of signatures legible. It will show you the difference between the random crisscross scratches that mark the bottom of a genuine piece of old glass and the too neatly parallel scratches that have been filed or ground into the bottom of a modern reproduction. Your magnifying glass will reveal the near-invisible knife scars that characterize most antique plates and platters, whether pewter or pottery. It will show you restorations in paintings, dates and mintmarks on coins, inscriptions on medals and countless other details that might go unnoticed by your less-well-equipped competitors. You won't have to look at the entire exhibition through your magnifying glass, but conveniently tucked away in your pocket, the glass will serve you so well on occasion, you'll be grateful to have it with you.

Take a tape measure along to the inspection. An ordinary tailor's measure that snaps back into a thin plastic wafer about the size of a fifty-cent piece will help you determine the exact width, depth and height of pieces you'd like to consider for your home, and whether or not they'll fit into the space that you have in mind for them. Most auction rooms will have a yardstick or a folding rule available, and you will usually be able to borrow it. But why not go prepared? You might want to check the dimensions of three or four different pieces in a single exhibition, but you might be reluctant to ask again and again to borrow the yardstick. Besides, I have yet to find an auction room that has more than one yardstick or rule available, and if there's a large crowd at the inspection—and frequently there will be—you may find yourself waiting your turn to use the magic wand. Of course, you can always wait until you see someone else measuring the piece in which you are interested, and then ask him for the dimensions. This is guaranteed to make a genuine hit! Immediately it lets him know that you share his interest in the piece, which automatically makes you "the enemy." Avoid alerting enemies and carry your pocket tape measure to the inspection.

Now, armed with steno pad, pen, magnet, magnifying glass and tape measure, you are ready to begin inspecting the items that will be put up for sale. Try to get a catalogue of the auction. There is an advantage in having all the lots listed and—to the degree to which they will be—described. If nothing else, the catalogue will give you a complete list of the sale, and you can check it over to be sure you didn't miss anything of interest. I like to work *from* the catalogue, looking up the items by lot number and then jotting down the numbers in which I am interested. In other words, I use the catalogue as my index to the exhibition, but I use my exhibition notes as my guide at the sale.

A catalogue may be free; it may cost a quarter, or a dollar, or several dollars. If the price is more than a dollar or two, the catalogue will probably be handsomely illustrated and filled with valuable descriptive information, and you will be buying a booklet worth keeping for reference.

If you are asked to pay a dollar for one of the two-sheet mimeographed lists that most auctioneers distribute free, or for which you might expect to be charged twenty-five cents, go ahead and buy one, but be aware that the management is probably out to wring every possible cent from the auction. It is just those lists that are so often found to be impressively full of little inaccuracies of description concerning condition, attribution, etc. Consider the catalogue purchase as a kind of ticket of admission and go to the auction as if you were going to a show—you will probably find it even more entertaining, because those last-ounce operators invariably give quite a performance. Don't expect to steal anything at such a sale, or you are liable to come away pretty disappointed.

The relative value of the catalogue to its purchase price is your first indication of the character of the auction. Like a good detective, you will want to consider it a clue, not hard evidence, that you have happened upon a treasure lode, a straightforward business enterprise or, alas, a den of thieves. You are going to find all three as you go from auction to auction. Happily for all of us, the first two greatly outnumber the third.

Being asked to fork over a dollar for a page-and-a-half mimeographed auction list (except if it is clearly stated that the proceeds from the catalogue sale are being contributed to a specific charity, school, organization, etc.) should serve as a warning that you have stumbled into the pirate's lair. If you have, don't panic. Go right ahead with the business of inspection. Try to be a bit more than usually thorough in your examination of any lot that interests you. Expect to find more than a little variance between your appraisal of an item and its catalogue description. Hold your estimated bid at a conservative level and don't under any circumstances allow yourself to be moved more than one bid beyond it. (All of us—and I mean *all* of us—exceed our bid ceilings from time to time, but no matter how much an auctioneer tries to run your bid, he cannot hurt you if you pull down your hand the instant the bid goes one over your established limit.)

How you proceed with the inspection will depend greatly upon how the auction lots have been displayed. I have found, oddly enough, that one of the hardest auctions to inspect is the Post Office auction regularly held in New York City. Except for clothing lots, which can be examined closely and may even be accessible for trying on, most lots at the Post Office auction are displayed in wire cages that will have you thinking you have wandered into the dog pound. The merchandise is carefully catalogued, but descriptions vary widely, and "damaged" can mean anything from a slight and inexpensively repaired dent in a silver coffeepot to a missing ear on a porcelain Fu dog or an impossible fracture in a crystal paperweight. Additionally, I have found that many of the Post Office auction lots are composed of so many items that it's impossible to do more than guess at the value of the contents of some of those wire bins. But for what little it is worth, inspection is essential at the Post Office auction, because when the sale begins, the lots are identified by number only, and you will find yourself really bidding blind if you have not at least taken a squint at the contents of the cages. I suppose the crowds and the lack of adequate space and supervisory personnel make it necessary for the Post Office to handle its auction exhibitions in this unhelpful manner, but for a nonprofit auction being held under the auspices of the postal service, the auctions are a strangely *un*-public service.*

Happily, most auctioneers are more generous than the postal service when it comes to letting you examine the lots they are putting up for auction. Remember, the exhibition is your time to look at the items on which you are going to bid. Do it then, and not, as one or two difficult types always seem to want to, while the sale is under way. There's nothing more annoying to the auctioneer, or to the audience, than to have someone stop the bidding cold while he requests the privilege of examining a particular lot. Some auctioneers will go along with this once or twice in the course of a sale. Some will permit special buyers the privilege that they deny to others. Most auctioneers are adamant about not allowing inspection to continue during the sale session. I stand with them. Eventually the bidder who interrupts the auction to request a quick look at an item, will turn the auction into a private exhibition at which almost every lot is subjected to his personal scrutiny.

Invariably, you will find that some of the more delicate items are displayed in locked cabinets. If you are interested in one of the pieces shown in a closed case, ask one of the at-

---

* They aren't the greatest bargains on the auction front either. Prices are decidedly not low—at least, they weren't at the last several sales that I attended —and while some of the lots are interesting, the general level of the offering is less than first rate. Bins filled with huge assortments of toiletries, books, kitchenware, household linens, etc., might be good lots for the owner of a small variety store, and I have seen some respectable radios and tape recorders at the Post Office exhibitions, but on the whole, these sales strike me as being overrated auctions where pretty inflated prices are realized.

tendants to open the cabinet and show you the item. Even if the key is in the door—and frequently it is—ask the attendant to open the cabinet for you and to remove the item that you want to consider. There are several reasons for doing this. For one thing, many of those display cabinets have doors that are difficult to open. Pull on them and you might find you have thrown the case and all its contents crashing to the floor. For another, most of the doors that aren't hard to open are difficult to close. The peril is different, but equally great; you might jar the cabinet just enough to knock together several little treasures. And you could wind up paying the appraiser's price for the items you break. The auction attendant will be familiar with the idiosyncrasies of the cabinet doors, and if he isn't—well, at least *you* won't have to make good on breakage. Additionally, if a piece is damaged when the attendant removes it from the case, there's no question concerning its condition when you handled it. Take it out yourself and you might have a little trouble explaining the chip in the base of that $100 Aurene goblet. It's a nuisance to have to ask someone to hand you each little item, but it is the right way to do it. For your peace of mind as well as his. Generally, most attendants will be glad to show you these things. If one does not seem to be, don't let it discourage you from asking to see any piece in which you are interested. Remember, the proprietor is going to want to see your money up close, so there's no reason for you to feel shy about wanting to see his merchandise when you go to the exhibition.

Most auctioneers actually prefer that you thoroughly inspect any lot before you place a bid on it. Most of them would rather have you pleased with your purchases and out spreading the word about the terrific buy you made at one of their sales—and coming back again to buy at the next auction. If you are disappointed, disgruntled, or defeated in your efforts to return an uninspected purchase, the auctioneer has lost a potentially good customer, and you have lost some of your enthusiasm for auction attendance. But all the goodwill in the world isn't going to make the auctioneer refund a purchase that you didn't bother to inspect before you bid for it. He's running a particular kind of sale, and you, as a buyer at that sale, are expected to live up to your part of the contract. It is in his interest as well as yours for you to make a thorough inspection of the items on which you intend to bid.

Watch out for the positioning of tags and stickers on the items you inspect. You will find that there are times when the identifying lot number has been pasted so that it conceals (what a coincidence!) a flaw. A careful look at the area around the tag will be your best clue to the possibility of damage beneath it. Except on the smallest items, scratches and cracks are likely to extend beyond the margins of a numbered sticker the size of a postage stamp. If you note the wispy ends of a scratch stretching from the margins of a sticker, expect to find greater damage just beneath the well-situated tag. Check the interiors of vases, cups and bowls. The reverses of platters and plates.

There's nothing wrong with giving a glass a tiny tap with your fingernail or even with the end of your pen—provided the end of your pen is not made of metal—to check for the ring of perfection.* Cracked pieces don't ring. A chipped piece, however, will. So check the edges for nicks, flakes and chips, even though the piece rings clear as a bell. And before you turn your inspection into something resembling a marimba concert, remember that lime glass (and a great deal of

* A pencil, by the way, is ideal for this—which is about the only reason I know for taking a pencil to the exhibition. You don't have to worry about the point. Rap once, *lightly*, with the wood. And be sure that you aren't holding the piece so that your fingers are muffling the tone. You can get the same effect with a small piece of dowel, a tongue depressor, a Good Humor stick or one of those little wooden rods from your child's Tinker Toy—in case, that is, you don't happen to have a pencil handy.

old glass—in fact, misconceptions to the contrary, some quite old American glass—is lime glass) doesn't ring with the bell-like tone of flint glass. If all you get is a dull "thunk," it could be that you are tapping a piece of lime glass that is in perfect condition. Flint glass seems, however, to have greater brilliance, so if the piece you are testing sparkles like flint and still goes "thunk," start looking for flaws.

Perfect porcelain rings. Cracked or mended porcelain will tell you its troubles in no uncertain terms. It answers your inquiring tap with a sound that almost articulates the word "crack." In inspecting glasses, bowls, vases, decanters, cups and other items of porcelain or glass, it is a good idea to carefully run your fingertip around the lip of the item and again around the base. You'll feel the slight roughness of chips you might not notice. You will also feel the difference in texture or finish in an edge that has been repaired or ground down. A cut-glass bowl with a chip in the rim will ring just beautifully. So will a crystal goblet with a nick in its lip. A fast circle with the finger will be your best guide to these most common defects. If you are inspecting a covered piece, don't forget to lift the lid and check the inside of the dish. Check the underside of the lid, too.

If you do not have time to inspect every item in a large lot —in a complete dinnerware service for twelve, say—pay special attention to those pieces that received heaviest day-to-day use. Look at the cups, the dinner plates, the saucers. Don't worry too much about the soup plates or the bouillon cups—those are the items you are least likely to find broken. I have seen dinner services in which the soup plates were the only perfect pieces. (I have twelve beautiful old soup plates that match a lot of useless broken dishes to prove it!) Look at the serving pieces, too. The soup tureen got used even if the soup plates didn't. Check the vegetable dishes and serving platters. The sugar bowl, cream pitcher and, if they exist (as they did in many proper Victorian dinner services), the teapot, coffeepot and water pitcher ought to be checked for chipped spouts and rims. Again, don't forget to remove the lids and inspect their undersides as well. Check the markings on items in a dinner service, too. There is a lot of gold-rimmed white china from Czechoslovakia, and superficially, some of it looks enough like Haviland to pinch-hit, here and there, for missing pieces— until, that is, you go to set your table with it.

Inspection is when you have time to count the goblets in a lot. Can you use eleven? Bear in mind that you will probably never find a twelfth. If eight or ten is the maximum you will want to seat at a formal dinner, you've got it made. Of course, if you have a chance to make a terrific buy, you always can have the host fill in with an old jelly glass—or better still, with that single elegant piece of Baccarat that you found in a box lot at another auction! Inspection is when you look for cigarette burns in the rugs, for rain stains on the draperies, for broken caning in the chair seats and backs,* for broken hinges, missing links, bent fork tines, threadbare needlepoint, signatures—promised or unannounced—and all the other qualities and qualifications that will affect your use of the item and its ultimate value.

There are many special inspection "hints"—as many as there are different kinds of auctions. An extensive library could be assembled devoted exclusively to identification and

---

* Don't forget to consider the cost of having them recaned when estimating the amount of your bid. I have found that the most reasonable and reliable cane work is done by craft guilds organized by the blind. You'll probably have to deliver and call for your chairs, but that inconvenience will be substantially offset by the fact that you will probably find the work completed quickly and by people who appreciate the chance to help you as much as you will appreciate their work. Good to remember if you need to replace woven rush seats, too. Recently some do-it-yourself plastic chair-caning kits have been introduced. If you happen to like the looks of the finished product, you might want to consider using them. Certainly they ought to serve perfectly well for an inexpensive chair you have bought for a child's room. But consider having real cane work done on your beautiful auction finds.

evaluation of antiques. You will find that you learn a great deal in the process of auction attending. And you will find that you begin searching the libraries and bookshops (and don't overlook the bookstands at the museums) for reference works covering periods and articles in which you are particularly interested. Happily, the renewed general interest in antiques has caused many excellent, long-out-of-print works to be issued again in inexpensive paperback editions, making it possible to build your own basic reference collection for less than $50. The same books would have cost you ten times that amount if laboriously assembled in original editions purchased from dealers in rare books.

Use your public library, too. And if a work you want, or a subject on which you would like to do more reading, is not in the collection: ask for it. Initially, I like to borrow the volume I need from the library. If I find that I have checked out the same book three or four times within a six-month period, I know that book is one I would profitably add to my personal collection, and at that point I buy a copy. There is so much duplication of information in book after book, and there are so many attractive books that sometimes add disappointingly little to one's knowledge, however much they may delight the eye, that a bit of prepurchase inspection is advisable. Don't neglect the boxes and cases of books that you will find put up at auction, either. Valuable reference works sometimes turn up where you least expect them.

Warman's Tenth Antiques and Their Current Prices (1970), E. G. Warman Publishing, Inc., Uniontown, Pennsylvania 15401, 493 pages, alphabetically arranged and indexed, illustrated, is a standard, amazingly comprehensive guide to current retail prices for an astonishing variety of antiques. One can learn a great deal more than values from a study of this handy little book. Anyone interested in antiques, at auction or elsewhere, should own this publication. Keep it handy in your car, or at your desk. It is useful in authentication and identification, and helpful in establishing your bidding maximums. But if you take it to the auction room during the exhibition or sale, you are identifying yourself as a tyro. Most of us ultra-cool types rush for the Warman book as soon as we have left the exhibition, even though we wouldn't dream of letting an auctioneer see us with it.

The Complete Antiques Price List (Third Edition, 1970), by Ralph and Terry Kovel, Crown Publishers, Inc., New York, is an illustrated listing of thousands of prices at which an astonishing variety of antiques have been sold. Edited and compiled with and/or by a computer, this volume makes a handy supplement to the Warman guide. The illustrations are of good size and quite clear. The number of prices that have been included is incredible. Although this book lacks the background information provided by the Warman guide, it more than compensates for that by alphabetically listing a volume of items too great for inclusion in the Warman format. I use both Kovel and Warman, and I recommend that any auction buyer do the same.

There are a great many books that deal with porcelain and pottery marks. Depending on the extent of your interest, some of the highly specialized works might be worth looking into. William Chaffers' *Marks and Monograms on European and Oriental Pottery and Porcelain* is a masterful and comprehensive work that has been revised several times and is currently available in a two-volume edition. Fully indexed, amazingly easy to use and featuring large, well-drawn examples of documented signatures, this book, which exceeds one thousand pages, is worth its not inconsiderable weight in gold. Even one properly identified auction purchase could represent a major saving on the book's current $25 retail price.

Here are some quick inspection hints that might help you more effectively appraise the lots on exhibition.

APPLIANCES

Like most auction lots, household equipment is usually sold "as is." And usually without benefit of service contracts, guarantees or other protections available to the original purchaser through retail channels. Occasionally, an auctioneer will declare an item to be "running," or "mint," or "operating perfectly." Most often, the buyer will have no assurance beyond the evidence of his eyes and ears, which in the case of television sets, radios, tape machines, stereo equipment, slide projectors, vacuum cleaners, electric fans and other similarly demonstrable articles, might be sufficient. How long the appliance can be expected to continue to operate is another matter entirely.

According to a report by the United States Department of Agriculture, most home appliances—including washing machines, dryers, refrigerators, electric and gas ranges, vacuum cleaners and automatic toasters—have a life expectancy of approximately fifteen years. Television sets are charted at eleven, nonautomatic toasters at seven. Electric sewing machines come in for an impressive twenty-four. Obviously, the use and care that equipment has received will affect the number of years that it will fall short of, or surpass, the "average." Appearance can give some indication of the kind of care that an appliance has received. And if you know that the average length of serviceability is fifteen years and that the appliance is only two or three years old, you can undoubtedly calculate a fair auction price that will leave ample margin for repairs, part replacements, etc. Bear in mind, however, that installation costs may boost the price of your auction acquisition. Consider the need for additional electric power, gas lines, special plumbing, new drains, exhausts, etc., which might run higher than if installation were completed by the vender. Consider, too, the cost of having your appliance delivered, if delivery would be in order.

On the positive side, most appliances bring ridiculously low prices at auction. Probably this is because most buyers are discouraged by that "as is" aspect of the sale. If you are in the market for a new whatever-it-is, or for a second or a third—an extra refrigerator, say, to use in the family room, or a vacuum cleaner to be kept upstairs—your unguaranteed auction purchase could be the answer. The major manufacturers of appliances maintain company-authorized repair services in most cities. If your auction-bought appliance is a fairly recent model —and I cannot think that you would deliberately acquire and expect to use a vintage one—the factory-authorized service will probably be able to supply needed parts and to guarantee repairs. At auction, I have seen three-year-old washing machines bought for $20. With an expected twelve additional years of service, they would seem to have been extremely good buys. A portable black-and-white television set that costs well under $200 new might be a poor auction investment at $10 if it required repairs, or a new picture tube, although a large console color television set that retails for more than $500, might be an excellent auction buy at $100, even if it required an equal expenditure for repairs.

AUTOMOBILES

Unless you are a professional mechanic, hire one to inspect the auto auction with you. Most of the auto auctions offer the services of a house mechanic, but (1) he is busy—maybe too busy to give you as much time as you would like, and (2) he *is* an employee of the establishment—a fact which, however meticulous he tries to be, must at least color his appraisal. Since you probably won't be getting any guarantee on your auction-bought automobile, invest part of the money you will save on your auction purchase in the services of a reputable mechanic, and *listen* to him. Most auto auctions positively gleam with Simoniz, new paint and polished chrome. Regardless of age, the cars will look terrific.

You will probably be allowed to start the car and to listen to the engine for a bit. I have yet to attend an auto auction that allows anyone to handle the cars in any sort of road test, which would seem to me the best possible method of inspection. The auctioneer will usually assure you that all of the cars were driven to the auction site—although he does not explain whether or not that was under their own power—which is meant to convince you, I suppose, that they do, indeed, run. And undoubtedly they do, for you will see them driven from the premises after being sold. If one of them balks, stalls, swerves and practically lies down to die at that point, it is up to the unlucky buyer to get it working before he can drive it away.

You can make a good buy at an auto auction, provided you buy a good car. In some large cities, you will find that retired police cars are put up for sale at auction. These vehicles, understandably, have a lot of mileage on them, but generally they have also been kept in good running order. Bidding on these cars is frequently lower than on similar models at the commercial auto auctions. I would think that as a first car for a new driver, one of these would make an ideal low-cost vehicle. These auctions are always listed in the newspapers, but the ads are so much smaller than those of the commercial auto-auction operations that you will have to make a special effort to look for them.

Even as not every car sold at auction is a lemon, neither is every car going to be a bargain. The spirit of competition is likely to be keen, especially if the bidding narrows down to a toss-up between two men. Check the prices of comparable cars at dealers' in your area. And in one of the publications that list current values for stock cars. Above all, be guided by the advice of your mechanic.

It is prudent to check the rules governing the sale at any auction, but it is imperative when you're buying at an auto sale. Be sure you completely understand the conditions of sale and, most important, the time at which (and *by* which) you must claim your purchase. If you have to arrange for insurance, registration, etc., be sure that you will have time to do it within the period allowed for removing your vehicle. The best time to find out is at the time of inspection. If you wait until the sale is under way, you might be too late. Some auto auctions reserve the right to resell any cars not removed from the premises within forty-eight hours. There may be others that allow only twenty-four. If the auction is held, as many of them are, on a Saturday, be sure to find out whether or not Sunday is considered part of that maximum privilege period. Inquire about garage fees, too—some car auctions charge them.

BOOKS, ALBUMS, MAGAZINES

If books, and similar lots such as magazines, postcards, Valentines and newspapers, are tied in bundles, packed in boxes, shelved or otherwise individually uninspectable, or if time does not permit detailed examination: *smell them!* That's right. If improper storage and dampness have led to mildew, the nose test will tell you immediately. Moisture is a great enemy of books. Remember, too, that if one leaf falls out, there is a more-than-excellent possibility that other leaves will soon follow suit. And if you want to be sure that you are adding only books to your library, look along the backbones of any old volumes—in between the curved binding and the sewn signatures—for signs of habitation. Tiny creatures can feast for years on a diet of paper, animal glue, vegetable dye and fabric, and that's what most old editions were made of. There are sprays and powders that will do away with the inhabitants, but it's easier all around just not to acquire them.

BRIC-A-BRAC

"Notice spelling," the importer's advertisement said. "We made it this way purposely—we do not wish to cheat anyone." It went on to point out that the porcelain reproductions that were being featured were absolutely accurate in detail (though a bit heavier in weight) except that the maker's name had been deliberately—if almost unnoticeably—misspelled. One of a pair of *s*'s had been eliminated (as in "Hesian" rather than "Hessian") from a well-known mark. This slight deviation from a famous signature is not uncommon. There is, for example, "Wedgewood" in addition to "Wedgwood," the latter being the one of value. Happening across some of these artfully missigned pieces among several hundred auction lots, one might just fail to take note of the slight variation in spelling, and bid in an imitation at a price that might be three times its cost and six times its worth. Signatures are important, and proper signatures are the only kind worth bidding for. Check them carefully, and if you don't recognize the mark, make a drawing of it and try to verify the signature before establishing your maximum bid on a piece.

Contemporary reproductions of popular antiques abound,

and quite a number of them find their way into auction rooms. (Quite a number of them find their way into antiques shops, too, which is a lot less understandable.) Some of the new copies would deceive only the most untrained eye. But many of them are so well done that they require expert appraisal. There's nothing wrong in selling them, or in buying them, as long as they are identified as copies and prices are adjusted accordingly. The time to find out whether a piece of glass or china is as old as you would like it to be is before you bid for it.

One test that involves no special training, although it requires a bit of research, is whether you see many similar pieces—either at auction exhibitions or in the antiques or gift shops or in your friends' homes. If there seem to be quite a number of whatever-it-is around all of a sudden, it certainly can't be considered "very old, very rare," no matter how the auction catalogue might describe it.

It has been said before, but it bears repetition: good things look good. They really do. Bad things sometimes look pretty good, and on the auction block, well lighted and glowingly described, they can look still better. So get accustomed to the look of quality that genuine pieces evidence, and if something doesn't just quite make it: reject it. Don't let the possibility of making a find tempt you into making a mistake.

MADE IN JAPAN is an unwanted identification on much pottery and porcelain. If the underside of a piece of bric-a-brac shows signs of MADE IN and there is some indication of ob-literation—it can be done with paint, acid, abrasives; even, occasionally, with ordinary household bleach, depending on how the legend was applied—99 times out of 100, JAPAN was what was removed. Look closely, in a good light, and you will undoubtedly see some traces of the word still lingering. Again, there's nothing wrong with owning these often quite decorative pieces if they happen to please you. Only don't bid for them as if you were acquiring an eighteenth-century European piece.

And while considering the mysterious Orient, don't confuse those meaningless shop marks with the proper signatures on antique pieces from China and Japan. Just because something has Oriental characters painted or impressed on its base, don't assume it to be Ming or Ching or anything of the sort. The ancient seal characters are showing up on quite new pieces. They look impressive, but most of them are as contrived as the plot of an old Fu Manchu novel, and some of them are probably not even as old. Sometimes Oriental objects are shown on little carved wood stands. This unquestionably makes them look more impressive, but it does not necessarily mean they ever graced the pavilions of the Forbidden City. New carved stands are being imported from Hong Kong and Korea and undoubtedly from other places. For the most part, they look thin and flat, and there is little or nothing of interest in the carving. A base of average size costs from $5 to $10 at an import shop, and should not add more than that to the cost of your auction purchase.

Since 1891, articles of foreign manufacture brought into the United States have been required to carry identification of country of origin. Like JAPAN, markings that thus would adversely affect an article's claim to antiquity (INDIA, for example on brass, CHINA on a twentieth-century piece that otherwise could masquerade as one of its ancestors) are sometimes covered or removed. Look for a variation in the finish of the base; for meaningless overpainting—a tiny gilt leaf, for instance, or a clumsy, overstuffed fleur-de-lis; a glaze that seems not to fit the general character of the piece—sticky, dead white or, perhaps, too lustrous; or indications that the original base has been removed (yes!) and replaced.

There are people who specialize in painting new marks on old china. The marks, though new, are usually intended to make the porcelain appear even older. Moral: Blue crossed swords do not necessarily a fine piece of old Meissen make.

Damages and repairs substantially affect the value of any article. Look for breaks and/or repairs at the edges of things. The fingers, heads, noses, chins, hat brims, shoe tips, skirt hems and coattails of figurines are the most frequent locales of wear and repair. If a repair is so well done that you cannot immediately spot it, you can adjust your bid accordingly. If three broken fingers will in no way diminish your pleasure in a little bisque shepherdess, by all means bid for her, but make note of her "as-is–ness." Look at the edges of flower petals, the tips of leaves. And check for missing or broken stems and branches. Check, too, for absent accessories. Was that little shepherdess holding a crook that has been chipped into a wand? Did the porcelain monkey musician once hold a drumstick? (Metal figures too have frequently lost part or all of some prop.) Ask yourself, "What's missing? How is this incomplete?" Often your next close look will supply the answer.

Many buyers are unaware that glass and china pieces can be mutilated into "mint" condition. Broken rims are sawed off, as are broken bases. Frequently the naked edge will be dressed with a bit of gold paint. When it is, the gold invariably looks quite different from any other gilt on the piece. A perfectly flat edge is a good indication, though not necessarily proof, of mutilation. Look at your fine porcelain and glass pieces. Notice the slight rounding of the lip? That's what you won't find on a piece that has been cut down. That someone thought enough of the piece to have it cut down does not prove value. It was valuable, perhaps, before it got broken. A mutilated piece may be worth less than one-tenth its perfect price. Look also to see if the design seems to stop abruptly at the flat rim. Does it make sense ending in that way? Or would it logically continue, to finish somewhere beyond the point at which the piece now terminates? Not many artists would have bothered to paint the feet of a dragon at the top of an urn, you know.

Look for missing finials, handles, covers and stoppers. Does the piece hint at being unfinished? Should it have a base? A cover? Feet? (If it has feet, does it have *all* its feet? And all the same feet?) Is it all original, or has it been assembled from diverse elements? (Stray vases sometimes wind up in metal mounts for which they were never intended. Some auction exhibitions abound in marriages not made in heaven—or, for that matter, in any factory or studio here on earth.)

Mounted pieces with felted bottoms, or affixed bases, are harder to inspect. Many otherwise desirable objects in porcelain or glass have been drilled for conversion into lamps. If the bottom has been covered with a carved stand or a circle of felt, look down through the top to see whether or not the piece has been drilled. (If you plan to use the piece as a lamp, you have no problem, except that you will want to reduce your bid for a drilled piece even though it happens to suit your purpose.) Sometimes you can feel the drilled spot through the felt. Put your finger on the center of the base and, with very slight pressure, trace gradually enlarging circles out toward the rim. If a wood or metal stand has been attached to the piece, see if there is an opening in the center of the stand. If there is a screw there, or an escape for an electric cord, you need no diagram to know to where it might lead.

The quickest way to distinguish between pottery and porcelain is to touch it. Porcelain feels cooler than pottery. Porcelain is also identified by its famous translucency, but not all auction rooms are sufficiently well lighted to make that test possible.

Learn to recognize the difference between fine hand painting and transfer-applied decoration. Your magnifying glass will help, but even before you reach for it, you will observe that transfer colors seldom have the "life" that paint imparts. Not all transfer pieces are bad, even as not all hand-painted porcelain is good. There is a lot of hand-painted turn-of-the-century china that ranks, in terms of merit, right up there with paint-by-number pictures. China painting was a popular hobby in Grandmother's day. Most of the work was done on Limoges blanks, and practically all of it was signed by the hobbyist. If a prominently placed name or set of initials is unknown, it is probably the signature of someone's maiden aunt or "artistic" bachelor uncle, and of no great significance, so don't bid more for it.

An abundance of new peachblow, Burmese, mother-of-pearl satin and millefiori glass has recently come onto the market. Antique examples of these famous art-glass pieces bring hundreds of dollars, and are listed accordingly in the various price guides. It is easy, therefore, to be tempted to bid for an auction lot described as "peachblow," "Burmese," etc. Before you bid, go look at a genuine piece of old peachblow, Burmese or whatever. Except for the satin glass, all the new pieces look dead by comparison—and most of the new satin glass will look pretty sick. The colors certainly fail to repeat the exquisite beauty of the originals, and the detailing of the new pieces is frequently clumsy, showing none of the fine work that characterizes the antiques. Don't expect photographs of old pieces to help you recognize new ones in this category. They will only confuse you. The reproductions look *exactly* like the pictures. What they don't look like is the real thing. Once you have seen that, you will never be tempted to overbid for a recent reproduction. The latest atrocities to emerge on the glass scene are imitation Tiffany pieces, some of which even carry imitation signatures. Again, go look at the genuine article and you will not be quickly taken in by a fake. Even the "original paper label" cannot be considered absolute proof of authenticity. New labels are being printed and affixed to both genuine and counterfeit pieces.

CHAIRS
(Antique)

Antique chairs are plentiful and frequently valuable. They frequently are also astonishingly *low*. There are several reasons for this. Wear (pure and simple wearing down of the wood) is one; another is that, strange as it might sound, in the eighteenth century, people *were* generally smaller. (Those little dollhouse rooms you see in museum restorations tend to be filled with furniture built to a smaller scale, which is one reason they look so especially charming to us present-day giants.) Eighteen inches is a comfortable seat height for a side chair. I've seen antique chairs that looked deceptively well proportioned with seats only fifteen inches from the floor. When in doubt, whip out the tape measure and check the distance from the floor to the front of the seat. If your heart is captured by a set of side chairs that fall short of the comfortable eighteen, you can have a couple of inches built onto them—but you will substantially diminish the value of your antiques and incur the cost of some possibly expensive reconstruction.

Everyone hears stories about the gifted handyman who took apart a wobbly old chair and completely refinished and rebuilt it, even managing to match a missing spindle, or to patch a bit of broken carving perfectly. Personally, I find these talented people few and far between. Unless you have the name of one of them securely tucked away in your address book (and maybe even on your Christmas list), it's a good idea to stay away from chairs requiring that kind of attention. There are, of course, such people, and some of them do beautiful work. Because of this—and probably because there are so many old chairs in need of their services—they can afford to be selective about what they will undertake. And about what they will charge. If needed repairs are extensive and at all delicate, don't laughingly assume that you can do them yourself. Check the cost of good professional work, and scale your maximum bid accordingly. If someone seems willing to bid higher for the piece, bear in mind that he might be doing the restoration himself—or if he is a dealer, he might be able to have the work done for substantially less than you would have to pay.

Check any chairs that you inspect for wiggles and wobbles. Remember: squeaks mean that something is loose. If the chairs are so displayed that you cannot touch them, at least look to see if all four feet of every chair actually touch the floor. Broken spindles aren't too bad, provided both pieces are present (and surprisingly often they are, tied with a bit of dirty white string, or wrapped together with a bit of wire). That's one repair you can probably do yourself. But check carefully for the missing spindle or the broken carving. It might sound impossible, but missing rungs are among the easiest defects to overlook when one is confronted by a jungle of gleaming mahogany. If you're involved with Victorian chairs with springs, padding, tufting, etc., your best bet is to test the seat, if you can, with a gentle but firm application of the hand. Look underneath, too, to see that the springs aren't leaking out like the curls of an inverted Medusa. And remember that fancy upholstery jobs involving tufting, buttons, etc., can cost more than the price of the chair.

Nineteenth-century reproductions of Queen Anne, Chippendale and other classic chair styles are frequently attractive and well made. And being one hundred or nearly so years old, they often have the rich, mellow look suggestive of the original. Usually the later pieces fail in terms of proportion, and construction differences will resolve any lingering doubts. There's nothing wrong with these now-antique copies of earlier antique pieces, as long as one doesn't buy them under the impression he is bidding for the astronomically priced originals.

CHESTS, CUPBOARDS, DESKS AND DRESSERS
(Antique)

Beyond making certain that the piece is complete, that all the wood is original, that the doors open and close and the drawers slide with reasonable ease, there isn't much to worry about in these pieces, except to be sure you are not paying an antique price for a reproduction. Some reproductions are extremely convincing. I find that the fastest thing to do is reach quickly behind the piece and touch the backboards. If they're thick, rough-dressed and wide, I take the examination a step further and start opening drawers.

Even the most carefully made reproduction will have drawer bottoms differing greatly from those of an original item. Plywood or fiberboard drawer bottoms are, of course, a dead giveaway. Drawer bottoms of smooth, thin wood are also indications of contemporary manufacture. Antique drawers had wooden bottoms that were thinned at the edges to fit into the drawer frame. You can identify the genuine article with your eyes closed; the tips of your fingers on the underside of the drawer will tell you everything you need to know.

Don't be too much impressed by dovetailed joints—almost all those reproductions are also dovetailed. There is a kind of joining that is characteristic of the seventeenth century, another that is typical of the eighteenth century, and another that quickly speaks to us of the machine age. Almost without exception, the earlier styles have been duplicated. Moreover, there are old pieces in which the drawers are not made with dovetail joints. Go ahead and look at the dovetailing—everyone does. But let the feel of the underside of the drawer tell you what you want to know about the possible authenticity of the piece. Of course, there are old pieces in which the drawer bottoms have been replaced, but not as many as you might expect. The same kind of test will tell you about the age of a cupboard with wooden doors.

The drawer pulls may look old and conform to the style of the piece, but if they are attached with machine-made screws, then call them not William and Mary, or Queen Anne. Recently at auction I saw a perfectly beautiful William and Mary–style lowboy, complete with shaped flat stretcher, pendant pulls and trumpet-turned legs. If I hadn't had a chance to examine it at the inspection, I might have thought I had stumbled upon a treasure. It was an incredibly good reproduction. Only the backboards, the drawer bottoms and the machine-made hardware spoke of modernity—as did the manufacturer's name, which I found stenciled inside one drawer.

It is not unusual to find a finial broken or missing from the ornamentation at the top of a tall cabinet or secretary. Consider removing the remaining finial(s) and using the piece without them. Only an antiquarian will know, and how often do you have one of them dropping in on you? Save the finials, of course, against the day you decide you want to sell the piece.

Age is not contagious. Just because you find a good many fine old pieces at an auction exhibition, don't automatically assume that everything else is sure to be old. One of the best ways to learn to distinguish between antique pieces and reproductions is to see a contemporary piece displayed alongside a fine old one. You'll be impressed at the difference in prices, too, once the bidding gets under way.

Be sure that the slant-front desk is in possession of both

rests, and that the wood is in good condition. Compartmented interiors are sometimes missing tiny drawers, dividers, doors or random bits of hardware. Check for split, or missing, drawer bottoms. And consider that one missing knob, or pull, might mean having to obtain a complete set of new hardware.

Have faith that a competent furniture restorer can probably correct anything that might be wrong with the piece—but at a price. Adjust your maximum offer to allow for it.

FRAMES
(On—or for—Pictures, Mirrors, etc.)

Look for missing ornamentation on old frames. Many an otherwise dandy buy has been reduced to a lemon by the absence of a leaf, cluster of acorns, bit of scrollwork, medallion, or whatever. If there is one in three of the frame's corners, there ought to be one in the fourth. Frequently there isn't. Some repair guides give instructions for making your very own casting from one of the existing decorations, and if you have a natural aptitude for such doings—include in that the refinishing of the entire frame in the event it becomes necessary to disguise some unfortunate results—you can acquire some attractive inexpensive frames and a whole winter of fascinating evenings for only a few dollars. On the other hand, if you don't want to wind up running "a little frame shop," look for missing detail and broken decorations on any frame that you inspect. You could, of course, consider removing the remaining decorations, but you would usually be removing much of the frame's elegance or charm, too.

The wood backing of old frames will frequently have dried and shrunk beyond the point of no return. Even if it doesn't look it, you will probably find it to be about as sturdy as old newspaper, and about as easy to tack down. Don't reject a good frame because the backboards are shot. And except for antique mirrors, on which the original wood back is desirable, don't think that the old backing adds substantially to the value or usefulness of a frame.

There are lots of cheap, new frames on the market, and occasionally they show up at auction. Most of them are pretty lightweight, which sometimes could be an advantage. Since they are inexpensive in the shops, they should bring even lower prices when they are sold at auction.

Don't assume that any frame can be hung any old way you fancy. Some have definite horizontals. Some have definite tops. Make sure that the design of the frame will permit it to be used in the way in which you want to use it.

Consider, too, whether or not you will be *able* to use it. If the wood is pulpy, you might have trouble getting screws and tacks to hold. Very narrow moldings split easily. Check the condition of the wood at the back of the frame, and save trouble by anticipating it.

If you are buying a frame for a particular picture or mirror, measure the frame's back to be sure it is large enough for your purpose, and measure its face to be certain it is not too large —unless, of course, you *want* to use a mat.

FURNITURE
(Contemporary)

Remember the scene in the film *Executive Suite* in which William Holden made his big pitch for the top job by delivering a ringing denunciation of the line of poorly constructed furniture the company manufactured in addition to its better-quality series? Well, like other elements in Cameron Hawley's story, that shoddy specialty line has its counterparts in what we blithely call "real life." Although it invariably sells at ridiculously low prices, this furniture, which is made primarily to be sold at auction, or at "Manufacturer's Close-outs," or through warehouse clearances, or "Inventory Sales," is often no bargain. No matter how attractive it might appear, it is usually a poor investment in terms of cost per year of use. Well-constructed furniture cannot be produced cheaply, and consequently, except under very special circumstances, it will not be sold cheaply. There are auction bargains to be found in contemporary furniture, but an exhibition filled with gleaming new pieces "direct from the factory," many of which prominently display price tags (usually impressively marked), is not the best place to look for them.

There are several ways in which you can distinguish a sale of good contemporary furniture from one based on shoddy "auction merchandise."

(1) The auction-line lots will usually be entirely "brand-new," and there will frequently be many examples of a single piece, varying, perhaps, in upholstery or finish. (In how many "decorator's showrooms" have you seen five identical chairs made up to display different upholstery treatments? Even the largest furniture outlets generally have only one finished piece and use fabric swatches to show alternate choices. Same goes for paints, stains, veneers, tabletops, tiles, mirrors, etc. etc. etc.)

(2) Ill-matched upholstery patterns are a sign of cheap production. Check the back of the piece as well as the front and sides, and don't forget the cushions. Both sides of the cushions if they are supposed to be reversible. Cutting each upholstery section so that the pattern will properly match that of the adjoining section is extravagant with fabric. You will find no such extravagance lavished on auction-line furniture. Carefully matched woods and wood grains can give you another indication of quality and craftsmanship not usually found in what the furniture trade calls a "promotional line."

(3) Cushions should fit snugly, conforming to the shape of the piece and to other cushions. Hanging threads, uneven welting and loose buttons are additional clues to inferior work.

(4) Cheaply made pieces will show cost cutting through the use of thin drawer bottoms and backboards; skimpy, light-weight, poorly detailed hardware; staples (yes!) and nails instead of screws.

(5) Good wrought-iron furniture is heavy, well joined and seldom in need of a trip to the welding shop.

Auction-line furniture has its uses—beyond, of course, the obvious purpose of making a profit for the manufacturer and for the auctioneer. Bid in at a realistic price, which means well below the retail price at which you might have purchased a comparable piece, it might serve perfectly well in a guest room where it would have only occasional use, or in a child's room where it might expectably be replaced in a few years. If furniture is wanted only for a limited period of time—a temporary residence, perhaps, or a student apartment—after which it will be expected to have neither use nor value, in-expensively made pieces can serve the purpose; but they should be inexpensively obtained. All too often, the excitement of buying at auction can lead to overpaying for something of inferior quality that would never have brought an equivalent price in a furniture shop.

When fine contemporary furniture is put up at auction, it is frequently a superb buy. If you come across pieces among diversified auction lots and they are in good, or redeemable, condition, you can sometimes buy at incredible savings.

If a piece is going to require new upholstery or refinishing, consider the cost of that work part of your purchase price, and adjust your maximum bid accordingly. Frequently an auction-eer will enthusiastically suggest cost estimates for such work. Not always are these in line with actual prices. Take time be-tween the exhibition and the sale to check the cost of comparable work in an upholstery shop or with a furniture re-finisher, and don't forget to add on, if the estimate doesn't include it, the cost of needed fabric, hardware or whatever. Restoration can double—even triple—the price of your auction purchase: which is not to say that the piece might not still be a terrific bargain. Only know beforehand approximately what additional costs you might be incurring. And if the auctioneer correctly points out that adding $10 worth of velvet will give you a $200 chair, remember that with web-bing, welting and whatever, the $10 worth of velvet can turn into a $75 upholsterer's invoice. Bid in at $100, that chair might or might not be a good auction buy.

The price an otherwise perfectly fine piece of furniture will bring at auction can be cut ridiculously low because of a minor scratch. With all the great retouching products on the market, it seems a little shortsighted categorically to reject a good buy because of a minor and often easily corrected defect.

The same applies to broken glass. Some broken mirrors and panels necessitate simple, inexpensive replacements, yet drastically reduce the price at which an excellent piece of furniture will be sold. If, however, the item that you are considering requires a new piece of glass in a special shape or color, bear in mind that replacement will probably not be any low-cost incidental.

House auctions frequently yield excellent offerings in furniture. But if the furnishings seem too new, too modern, too abundant, too large or too elegant for the residence from which they are being sold, consider the possibility that they might be auction-line pieces brought in for the sale; inspect carefully, and bid accordingly. Or if the furnishings of one or two rooms seem strikingly out of character with those of the rest of the house, consider that the family, perhaps, decided that they would not sell the contents of certain rooms, and the auctioneer filled the gap with inexpensive promotional pieces, for which he expects to achieve improved prices by selling them in conjunction with better lots.

FURS
(Apparel)

Fur coats, jackets, stoles and capes frequently show up at auction, and as with all other kinds of auction lots, you can make a good buy—*if* you buy something good.

Don't buy on impulse. Inspect the garment as carefully as you would if you were buying from the town's most exclusive furrier. In fact, inspect it *more* carefully. If you are offended by the idea of wearing secondhand furs—and there are many who are—don't expect the money that you save by buying one at auction to miraculously change your attitude. It probably will not. Be honest enough to admit to yourself that that is how you feel, and leave the bargains to the next bidder. No matter how inexpensively something is acquired, it is an extravagance if wearing it makes you feel shabby rather than splendid.

Certainly you will want to check the seams and stress points of any fur garment, and the most obvious places for signs of wear—all edges, the armholes, the undersides of the sleeves, pocket flaps, belts, and the areas around any fastenings. If you can, look under the lining to see the condition of the skins. Tapes and clamps are signs that the skins have become too dry and brittle to permit lasting repairs to be made with needle and thread—and that alteration or restyling would probably be difficult or even impossible. If the lining is tacked down so that you cannot see the skins, listen closely as you close your fist over a patch of fur and try to wrinkle it. If the skins are severely dry, you will hear a scratchy sound like that of paper being crumpled. The stiffness or suppleness with which the fur moves at your touch will give you another clue to the condition of the skins and the kind of care they have been given.

You might be able to learn something about the age of the garment by considering the lining. A brand-new lining is usually a sign of an older fur, unless the styling and appearance of the garment also live up to the new look. A worn lining not only dates the garment, but also suggests the amount of service it has seen and that, of late, it might not have been out too often. Given proper care, however, a good fur garment should be wearable for many, many years.

Raccoon is one of the longest-wearing, most durable furs, which is all very nice if you happen to want raccoon. Mink, seal, muskrat and beaver tend to wear well, and would represent better used-fur investments than would a garment of the same vintage made from squirrel, broadtail or nutria.

If several fur garments are included in an estate auction, consider whether or not they would logically have belonged to a single owner. Size, style and lack of duplication would be reasonable criteria. The owner of three fur coats, a jacket, a stole and a shrug *probably* gave less wear and better care to her furs than did the lady with one all-purpose mink. Chances are that that single mink wasn't in the same luxury league with the other woman's several furs, either.

Many fur garments have the owner's name or monogram embroidered on the lining. These identifications are usually heavily satin-stitched and tedious to eliminate by pulling out the threads. If the several furs that you are inspecting carry the same name or initials, you can be fairly certain that— most recently, at least—they belonged to a single owner. Garments lacking this identification might have been relined for purposes of resale, which could indicate that the original lining was worn out—meaning that the furs have seen heavy service, or received improper storage or care. Or they might be sample garments. Or unclaimed orders. If you notice an odd little patch pocket, or a peculiarly placed label tacked to the lining, peek behind it to see if it is not covering an embroidered name or monogram, or the telltale tracks of one that was picked out thread by thread.

Woven labels are so easily switched from garment to garment and tacked onto linings for which they never were intended that, like many porcelain markings, they are most convincing only with the overwhelming confirmation of the article itself.

Some of the fashion world's most glamorous names line their creations with special fabrics featuring woven repeats of their famous signatures. Check to see that the lining perfectly fits the garment in which you find it, and that the whole garment shows the kind of careful workmanship that you would expect from a designer whose name alone will substantially enhance the price.

Good furs have uniform color and texture and, in a well-made garment, will have been carefully matched. Be sure that inferior skins were not used as hidden economies under a collar or sleeve, or where they would be concealed by fastening.

And make trying-on a part of your inspection of any fur apparel on which you are considering placing a bid. Ask the auctioneer or the attendant if you may try on the fur. Let him help you with it, if he wants to. But feel the fit, and see how you look in the garment, before you buy it—because if you win the bid for it, remember, it is yours. If the auctioneer discourages you from trying on the fur, or flatly refuses your request: skip it, and buy a better fur at some other auction.

JEWELRY

Only training, experience and, in certain instances, some fairly complex laboratory equipment can ensure the accurate appraisal of gemstones. Maybe experts can distinguish between natural and cultured pearls by complicated mechanical tests, and maybe by running a strand of pearls across your teeth, you can tell the smoothness of cheap simulated pearls from the irregular surfaces of cultured and natural pearls, but such tests are hardly practical at an auction exhibition. Synthetic (man-made) emeralds and natural emeralds are the same in practically all respects except price, and just about impossible to tell apart without laboratory tests and a well-trained eye. Large gem rubies are more expensive than diamonds of the same size. Large sapphires of the same quality cost substantially less, yet rubies and sapphires are both corundum gems and could not be distinguished one from the other by someone who was color-blind. Beads of genuine amber will float in seawater, but that's another test you could not introduce at most auction exhibitions.

One thing you can do, of course, is know from whom you are buying jewelry and on what terms. I know one auctioneer who uses the word "genuine" in cataloguing any piece of jewelry that he absolutely guarantees. Lots sold without that designation are offered "as is," and might consist of natural, synthetic or imitation stones. What they definitely are not is returnable. It is up to you to know precisely how any jewelry lot in which you are interested has been catalogued and what, if any, guarantee that description conveys. Notwithstanding the customary disclaimer of responsibility, most auctioneers will refund the price of jewelry that was inaccurately described. Remember, though, that they are probably not legally required to do so—which means that if you do not know your gemology, you had better be sure that you know your auctioneer.

A gentleman who, for several years, supervised a major loan society's monthly auctions of unredeemed jewelry reports that both private purchasers and dealers were able to buy consistently well at those sales. Both the society's representatives and the auctioneer's staff were committed to giving accurate appraisals and responsible estimates to help the private buyer effectively compete with the better-informed professionals. "We practically used to take people by the hand," recalls my friend, "and in the course of one exhibition, we would give them a pretty fair idea of what to look for when evaluating a piece of jewelry." Not every auctioneer, however, is equipped —or inclined—to provide such service. Some will give deliberately low estimates in order to encourage attendance and stimulate bidding. Others will quote inflated appraisal figures because they want to enhance the presumed value of their offerings—which, if the pieces are bid in for much less, gives the impression that tremendous bargains are to be found at their sales. Some auctioneers simply are not competent to appraise jewelry and will admit it. Some aren't and won't. If you happen to attend an exhibtion such as those my friend formerly supervised, not only could you buy with confidence, you also might learn quite a lot about jewelry.

But suppose you don't?

If you plan to bid for something important, you might ask a professional appraiser, or a jeweler, to attend the exhibition with you. If you don't have an appraiser on tap, and your yellow pages fail to yield any, ask your insurance agent to recommend someone. Expect to pay an appraisal fee. If the charge seems steep for the few minutes it might take to evaluate a piece of jewelry, remember that you are also paying for years of training. Only the goddess Minerva came into the world fully armored with wisdom. Everyone else has had to work at it.

Be suspicious of terrific bargains in jewelry. There are not many to be found. Fine gems, while seldom offering spectacular promise of appreciation, are amazingly stable investments, and have consistent negotiable value throughout the world. No one—auctioneers included—knowingly lets them slip through his fingers. At auction, your best opportunity to get a fine jewel at a fraction of its worth is to find one hidden away in an old trinket box, or in a locked drawer of a dresser, or amid the contents of an old trunk, or wherever someone once put it for safekeeping and let it be forgotten. And does that happen often? Not very. Of course, you can sometimes buy jewels at less than the retail price by outbidding one of the dealers in the audience—as long as you know that the pieces for which you are competing were not consigned by your opponent. Bear in mind, however, that some dealers in jewelry will work astonishingly close to the line, often taking only a small profit on each of many quick sales. Accordingly, you cannot calculate that because Dealer X bids up to $750 for a piece, you will secure a wonderful bargain by giving the next advance. You might, but also, you might not. It all depends on the piece.

Natural, synthetic and imitation stones are used in jewelry. *Natural gems* are those formed by the forces of nature and include the four precious stones—diamond, ruby, sapphire and emerald—and the various semiprecious stones—opal, topaz, jade, turquoise, garnet, tourmaline, lapis lazuli and some sixty more of earth's twelve hundred mineral species. *Synthetic gems* are made by man in the laboratory and duplicate natural stones in chemical composition, physical properties and appearance. There is an important distinction to be made between synthetic and "simulated" stones. A synthetic gem is a genuine stone in every respect and, although somewhat less costly than its natural counterpart, has definite—often substantial—value. It can be told from a natural gem only by expert examination. A simulated stone is an *imitation gem,* fashioned from glass, plastic or other inexpensive material, and has, at best, some ephemeral decorative value. It is possible to find imitation stones set in precious metal, or to purchase an antique piece in which natural, synthetic and imitation stones are combined—the more recent synthetics and imitations having been added to replace missing stones.

Pearls are organic gems that belong in a class by themselves, if only because some authorities classify the pearl as a precious stone, while others insist that it is only semiprecious. Like the mineral gemstones, pearls can be separated into three categories. Oriental, or *natural, pearls* are the most precious. Having been formed about a minute particle that generally decomposes, most natural pearls consist of nothing but layer upon layer of nacre. *Cultured pearls,* while not precisely manmade, are at least man-induced, since they result from the insertion of a bead core into the pearl oyster, which, during the next three or four years, obligingly covers the bead with approximately one millimeter of nacre. The size of a cultured pearl depends largely on the size of the implanted bead, and not, as with a natural pearl, upon the thickness of the deposited nacre. Cultured pearls of fine quality have great beauty and considerable value, and might bring from 10 percent to better than 20 percent of the price of comparable natural pearls. *Simulated pearls* are imitations that have been coated with iridescent "pearly" lacquer. Depending on the depth of the lacquer coating and the care with which the product is made, simulated pearls can be quite attractive, but attractiveness is their chief value.

There are four principal factors to consider in evaluating a gemstone: size, color, perfection, and the way in which the stone is cut.

Size is a matter of record in most auction catalogs. Most gems are measured by carat weight. Diamond weights in the intermediate range between carat sizes are given in points, and since there are one hundred points to the carat (exactly like one hundred cents to a dollar), it's clear that, for example, a catalogue listing for a "2.75 ct." diamond means a 2¾-carat gem. Some people think that a 20-point diamond means a stone having twenty facets. It doesn't. It means the diamond weighs one-fifth of a carat. A 20-point diamond might sound pretty massive to the uninformed, but actually is too small to be considered for, let us say, even the most modest single-stone engagement ring. Pearl weight sometimes is expressed in grains, there being four grains to the carat. A pearl described as weighing 8 grains might sound negligible. Think of it as equivalent to a 2-carat gem and you might want to take a better look.

Color greatly influences the value of a gemstone. A distinct yellow or brown tint is undesirable in a diamond. "Blue-white" is the term most frequently used to describe diamonds that either are colorless or (in very rare cases) have a faint suggestion of blue. Those are the stones to look for, but they constitute only a small fraction of the diamond world. Most diamonds have some off-color (slightly yellowish) tint, including some of the best one can buy. What you are trying to avoid is a *distinct* yellow-to-brown tinge. (Paradoxically, there are a few genuinely "fancy yellow" diamonds with a deep, pure yellow color, and these can be very rare and expensive stones. They occur so infrequently, and are such a special taste, that you can on the whole disregard this point as being interesting but academic.) Try to examine diamonds against a white background, and away from objects that might lend them reflected colors. If the exhibition provides only colored cloths as backgrounds, use a white handkerchief, or a sheet of white paper, under the stone when you want to evaluate its color. More important than the size of a pearl are its color and luster. Color, including brilliance of iridescence, is the most significant feature of an opal. A rich, blood-red color can make a large ruby worth ten times the price of an equally large sapphire, although both are corundum stones. A pink sapphire is not considered a pale ruby, yet only a slight color gradation distinguishes the two.

Perfection means absence of flaws—freedom from interior cracks, fissures, black carbon spots, impurities, clouds, etc. Diamonds, as everyone must know, are the hardest substance on earth, and consequently are not readily scratched and nicked. This is one reason the diamond is ideal for setting in rings, bracelets and other jewelry in which softer stones might become scarred. The Mohs scale is a table of relative hardness ranging from 10 (diamond) to 1 (talc) on which each substance will scratch any material of equal or lower number. Rubies and sapphires rank 9 on the Mohs scale, but are a great deal less hard than diamonds. Emeralds may vary from 7.5 to 8, with synthetic emeralds consistently being the harder. Amber ranks a soft 2.5, which means that your fingernail could probably scratch an amber buckle. A jeweler's loupe is needed to detect internal flaws that would cause a stone to be considered slightly, quite, or very imperfect. Few amateur appraisers are capable of such hairline distinctions, which is another reason why substantial purchases should be given the benefit of expert consultation. Some authorities insist that there is no entirely perfect gem, and that stones must be evaluated in terms of their relative imperfection. This is certainly true of the emerald in particular. Interior flaws are so characteristic of both natural and synthetic emeralds that makers of simulated emeralds often imitate the fine lines and cracks in their fabrications!

Cutting, when properly done, reveals the stone's maximum brilliance and beauty—sometimes at the cost of much precious material. A modern "brilliant cut" achieves this best. A diamond cutter might sacrifice half, or more, of a stone's weight to complete a brilliant cut (round shape when viewed from above, faceted above and below the girdle [equator] of the stone), but in the process, he will greatly increase the diamond's value. An emerald-cut (square or rectangular) diamond of less than three carats is not as expensive as a brilliant-cut stone of the same size because the emerald cut allows a greater yield from the rough diamond. Because of the popularity of the emerald cut for larger stones, however, emerald-cut diamonds of three carats or more will equal or surpass in price brilliant-cut stones of the same weight. Marquises (long, pointed ovals), hearts, and other special shapes usually necessitate the loss of even more than half of the rough stone, and so can be proportionately more expensive. But the brilliant-cut is the basic diamond, and in judging its worth, experts emphasize the importance of proper cutting, since it governs the path of light through the stone and the manner in which it reflects from surface to surface to give the gem its fiery brilliance. Brilliant-cut stones that are cut too shallow, or too deep, are depreciated in value just as if they contained flaws. Rose-cut (flat base, faceted dome top) diamonds were widely used in Victorian jewelry. They are generally much less valuable than brilliant-cut stones, and while they can possibly be recut, the work is not cheap, and the size of the stone will be substantially reduced.

Other factors can influence the prices that certain pieces will bring at auction. Jewels with important historical or celebrity associations have value beyond the intrinsic worth of the stones. Stones mounted in settings designed by famous jewelers also will command increased prices. Fashion trends in semiprecious stones can greatly influence their popularity and, consequently, their prices. Interestingly, the introduction of synthetic gems has not diminished the worth of or interest in natural stones.

There are more tests for faked jewels than there are types of faked jewels. One of the most common deceits is a sort of gem sandwich known as a doublet, when it is made up of two components, or a triplet when it has three. A doublet might have a top layer of good stone laminated to an inferior base to give the appearance of a larger, more valuable gem. If the lamination does not show when the stone is viewed through a jeweler's loupe, it may be necessary to have a suspected doublet X-rayed. Triplets might have a colored center layer giving character and brilliance to a pair of otherwise undistinguished stones. Such a construction will sometimes reveal itself when the jewel is examined from the side. False cameos are made from two stones of different colors. Careful inspection will frequently reveal the figural carving to have been glued to a smoothly polished stone back. A true cameo is a single stone slab in which the relief figure results from artful carving away of parts of one layer of color to expose a contrasting shade. The "cameo" one most frequently encounters is merely a shell of thin construction, rather than the much more valuable substantial slab.

Perhaps the simplest test—and one that you can make at an auction exhibition—to distinguish gems from glass is to touch the stone to your cheek. If it feels cool, and remains cool for some time, this is some slight indication that it is a genuine crystal. Glass might feel cool on contact, but will quickly lose its cool, as will most plastics.

Even if you're only inspecting pieces of costume jewelry, don't forget to check for missing stones.

LAMPS

In estimating your maximum bid for any used electrical fixture, reduce the offer by $5 and prepare to rewire the piece. If you have to consider complicated rewiring, or replacement of a special (nonstandard—perhaps European, or outmoded) socket or switch, allow at least $10 and plan to have the work done professionally. Even if the lamp is illuminated when you see it on exhibition, if the wire is anything but brand-new, replace it before you try to use the fixture in your home.

Unless, of course, you actually enjoy the excitement of show-
ers of sparks, smoldering, fumes and possible blackouts. Tiny
breaks in the insulation on an old cord can set off a regular
little Fourth of July. If you happen to be holding the piece,
not only could you be hurt, but you might drop and break
your new lamp. Avoid accidents and disappointments—rewire
first!

Since you are going to rewire anyway, there's little point in
worrying that many of the old fixtures you find on exhibition
will have had their cords nipped off. Some people seem to find
a frayed cord terminating in an aging plug to be more reassur-
ing than a bit of clipped wire. Why bid more for a length of
cord that you are going to replace?

Leaded glass shades and glass panel shades are currently
so popular that many marriages of a base and shade never
intended for each other are solemnized at the auction block.
One popular combination involves fitting a ceiling-drop
shade onto a table-lamp base. If you happen to like the effect,
at least check to see that the shade's shallowness, or flare,
does not leave the light bulbs exposed when the lamp is set at
table height. Many glass lampshades look quite different when
not illuminated. If possible, try to see the shade both with and
without light. If the lamp on which the shade is displayed
is not working, ask to have the shade removed and held over
a lighted bulb. If the lamp is working, ask to have it turned
off. One of the most beautiful decorated glass shades that I
have ever seen was unbelievably ugly when it was not illuminated. How disappointed the buyer must have been if
he failed to see it that way during the auction exhibition! His
lamp was a night-blooming knockout, all right, but by day it
must have been an eyesore. I can't imagine how much I
would have bid for that lamp if I had not first seen it with
the light off. Disappointment sometimes lies in the other direction, too. Once, before I had learned to look at shades

both with and without light, I bought a lamp with a shade of beautiful green glass panels. At the flick of a switch, the richly glowing green faded out into a milky, tainted white. I finally recaptured some of the color by using yellow bulbs in the lamp. The result isn't quite what I had originally wanted, and it is certainly no reading light, but since the lamp was a nonreturnable auction purchase, it's a compromise I've had to accept.

If you are curious as to whether a particular glass shade belongs to the base on which you find it, check the fit. The shade should not spin, sway, sit at a slight slant, or do anything else suggestive of improvisation. Those lamps, even when mass-produced, were never made that sloppily. Remove the finial or other mounting and see if the shade has not been installed in some makeshift manner.

Scenic shades featuring landscapes painted on the reverse should be seen illuminated, not only so that you can fully appreciate their beauty, but also so that you can check for thin spots where paint might have flaked off, or fading.

Most broken glass panels are easy and inexpensive to replace. Exceptions: (1) a color difficult to match, (2) an unusual curve to shape. Replacing broken tiles in a leaded shade will probably require the services of an expert, no matter what the auctioneer might suggest concerning the simplicities of epoxies, solder or the like.

Look up under the shade of any lamp with a socket switch to be sure you can reach it comfortably. (Yes, I know about toggle switches, but maybe you won't want to add one.) If there is a chain socket, try it a few times to make sure the lamp doesn't need to be steadied every time the light is turned on or off. (Yes, you probably could have a switch socket installed, but there are lamp designs for which only a chain socket is practical.)

If the lamp that you are considering is being sold without

a shade, bear in mind not only what a new shade will add to the cost of the lamp, but also how much it might increase its height.

PAINTINGS

The most spectacular auction sales usually involve works of art. Great discoveries, record prices, the sale of a famous work from a private collection frequently puts auction news on the front page. Today, buying art at auction is more popular than it has ever been. The continuing rise in prices of paintings and graphics has brought new collectors into the field, and new buyers into the auction room. And the suddenly ubiquitous "art auction" has placed "original works of art" within the reach of a growing number of eager buyers who probably would never have wandered into an exhibition, or purchased a painting off a gallery wall.

Many factors can contribute to the price of a painting, but primarily it will be determined by (1) the quality of the work itself, (2) the reputation of the artist, (3) the authenticity— established or doubtful—of the work. Appreciation of quality is a matter of taste, judgment and knowledge. An artist's reputation can be established through a bit of library research. Authentication, however, takes a bit of doing.

There is a commonly accepted code that is used in many catalogue descriptions to indicate varying degrees of certainty in regard to authenticity. The use of the artist's full name, completely spelled out, is an indication that there is substantial confidence in the genuineness of the work. Use of the artist's last name and first initial only suggests probability. Use of the last name alone would generally be a sign of doubt.

Additionally, there are those confusing modifications such

as: "in the manner of," "school of," "attributed to," and "after." Usually these are not niceties. They say exactly what they mean. Which, in the case of "after," can mean that a painting is a later (perhaps even modern) copy of a famous artist's work.

Size is really no indication of value, although a large canvas by an artist will usually be expected to realize a better price than one of his smaller works might bring. But quality means more—not only in terms of worth, but also in terms of the enjoyment you will derive from the painting.

Don't judge a painting by its frame. And don't add value to the picture because you see it displayed in a lighted frame. That little lamp adds light to the canvas, and perhaps a few dollars to the cost of the frame, but it makes *no contribution whatsoever* to the worth of the painting. It is the easiest thing in the world to have a fine painting mounted in an illuminated frame. You can do it too—*after* you have acquired a fine painting. Some of the most unfortunate paintings that I ever have seen exhibited at auction have been the most elaborately framed. Some of them have brought high prices while beautiful and interesting unframed works were ignored. If a fancy frame is what you want: look for a frame. But if you are going to buy a painting: look at the painting, and remember that everything else is just so much window dressing. Of course, if a picture that you want happens to be wearing a frame that you like, and there is a lamp over it (and you have a suitable electric outlet where it can be connected once the painting is on your wall), don't let those fortunate extras stand in your way. Only remember that they are extras, and not indices of value.

Varnish, shellac and a light coating of glue can add years to the appearance of a painting. Shrinking as it dries, glue will leave a crackled, antiquelike surface that can be mistaken for genuine age. No sense adding more than the cost of a bottle of glue to the price that you would pay for a painting that has been so treated. If, that is, you want to consider buying it at all!

You can learn something about the age of a canvas—the fabric itself, if not the painting on it—by looking at the back. If you can look at it against the light, you also can spot tiny holes, tears, patches and repairs that might not show under the paint. Plenty of new pictures, however, have been painted on old canvas—sometimes right over older and better paintings. Besides, the age of a painting adds very little to its quality. Bad art does not get any better even after two or three hundred years. In fact, since it might not have been very much appreciated, an inferior painting usually arrives on the auction block in far less satisfactory condition than age alone could account for.

Suspect works attributed to famous names that turn up at out-of-the-way auctions. No matter how interesting the story may be of the now-destitute collector who has at last been reduced to parting with his greatest treasure for a fraction of its worth, it is probably not true. If it is, then the ultimate treasure is probably not authentic. Forgeries and fakes have found their way into famous collections too, you know. The whereabouts of most of the known works of the world's great painters are a matter of well-kept record. In *Chapter 5: How to Make a Killing* is the story of the Gauguin table that was sold at auction for $20. But I have yet to hear of any of Gauguin's paintings being sold in that way. Suspect, also, your own miraculous "finds." Chapter 5 describes my "Rembrandt" etching, and its disappointing aftermath, so that, hopefully, you will never have reason to relate a similar auction story.

Assembly-line techniques are being employed to turn out an astonishing number of "original oil paintings" for sale at auction and through specialty shops. These uninspired, mass-produced "works of art" frequently bring low prices, but are of such abysmal quality that one would be much better advised to acquire a good original graphic.

Every expert to whom I have spoken has stressed the importance of buying what *you* like. Don't expect to make a killing. Don't buy a picture because you fancy it to be a lost masterpiece. Don't "invest" in some hot new name that might very quickly go cold. Don't overbid because you recognize your principal competitor to be a dealer: he may already own the picture for which he is bidding. Buy the painting that you like, regardless of its current "in" or "out" status. If it pleases you—if it moves, delights, inspires, or provokes a genuine emotional or intellectual response—then it is a picture for you to own and enjoy. Which, in this highly subjective area, just might be the only valid bit of inspection advice anyone could follow.

RUGS

The floating auction of Oriental rugs is often a magic carpet to disappointment. Some of those highly advertised caravans of carpet values that crisscross the country, temporarily setting up in hotel ballrooms, motel meeting rooms, lodge halls and clubhouses, specialize in selling inferior merchandise at distinctly superior prices. If you plan to acquire a beautiful Oriental rug—whether you are going to buy a fine antique, a used rug, or a brand-new one—you will do well to consider the credentials of any vender from whom you contemplate making the purchase. And don't mistake repetition for reputation. Just because some circulating shill show regularly stops in your community, don't assume that it consequently must be all right. Maybe it is. Or maybe what is all right is the kind of customers that grow in your neck of the woods—and the kind of money they are willing to spend.

Some of the vagabond merchants carry one or two really fine carpets which actually will be sold if a proper price is reached; but the bulk of the offerings frequently consists of mediocre—or worse—merchandise, which, by clever manipulation and the always-reliable stimulus of competition, is disposed of at prices far higher than those at which comparable —or better—carpets could be bought at retail. Why spend more than you need to for something that might well be less than you thought, just because some auctioneer dons a fez or a turban, uses an exotic name, and once or twice a year passes through your town with a van full of rugs? Unethical operators peddling their wares in this manner do much to undermine public confidence in buying at auction. There's nothing wrong with buying a rug at an auction—I've done it myself and, hopefully, will again; it is *which* rug you will buy at *what* auction that can make the difference between a well-priced purchase that will give you years of enjoyment and beauty and an overpriced lemon that will give nothing but trouble and regret.

Shop the rug merchants in your area and develop a familiarity with prices, bearing in mind that age, condition, size, pattern, and any number of other factors will account for much variation from store to store, and from carpet to carpet.

Decide in advance what kind of rug you want. What color scheme will suit the room in which you plan to use it. What pattern. And what size not only will fit the room, but will look proper in it. A rug is nothing to buy on impulse. Hopefully, you are going to use the rug for many years. That gives you a long time in which not to like it. Know what you want first. Then set out to find it.

There are two kinds of auction at which, on the basis of *careful* inspection, you can bid with confidence for the rug that meets your previously defined specifications. One is a sale at which you have observed rug dealers among the active buyers. The other is an estate auction, provided you know the carpets in which you are interested *were* part of the estate. Of course, not every carpet in every mansion was a winner, you know. All of us make mistakes—and that goes for some of those millionaires who spent fortunes for floor coverings.

It is easy enough to recognize the rug dealers in an auction audience. Most often they will arrive just in time to bid for the lots in which they are interested. Usually they will cluster around the carpets and examine them briskly without turning their inspection into a three-act play. They'll look at the back; flip a corner over, perhaps; give the rug a quick shake, and bid or retire, depending on how they find the offering. Most rug buyers act with dispatch. There is seldom any of the "maybe-I-will, maybe-I-won't" backing and forthing characteristic of many nonprofessional bidders. Attend a number of auctions at which carpets as well as other lots are sold and you will soon learn who the dealers are and where and what they buy.

Estate sales often include desirable carpets, but not infrequently additional rugs will be brought in, to augment the sale and to enhance the appeal of merchandise that otherwise might be less readily disposed of. If the rugs are shown on the premises of the estate, you at least have the advantage of seeing whether or not they fit the rooms. I remember one exhibition we attended at which the borders of a huge Oriental carpet had acutally been turned under so that it would squeeze into the room in which it was displayed. No owner in his right mind would ever have treated a rug in that way. And if he had been so foolish, he would have needed a doctor in permanent residence to attend to the sprains and fractures that would have resulted from all the tripping. Plus which, if the carpet had been used in that manner, it would have shown greater wear on the ridges over the folded-under edges. At that same exhibition, we noted several small rugs used to cover an upstairs hall that connected four bedrooms and led to a staircase. A runner might have been convincing, but those closely scattered rugs made no sense at all in what must have been a busy traffic area.

Color and quantity are other indications as to whether carpets were owned or have been added for the sale. If a fine rug seems unrelated to the other furnishings, there is a good chance that it never lived with them. An exhibition of more rugs than the house could conceivably accommodate should certainly suggest that something has been added—unless you know that the owner happened to be a rug collector, or a dealer.

A disadvantage of inspecting carpets in the rooms in which they were used is that furnishings can conceal faded areas, stains, worn spots and other defects. And sometimes the light is simply not adequate for proper appraisal.

Many exotic and some familiar names are used in conjunction with carpet sales. Dealers and collectors use them freely, and you and I may sometimes enjoy salting our conversation with references to "Sarouk" or "Kirman," but quality and condition so greatly govern the price at which a rug will be sold that, except for the rarest of the rare, which you need not often expect to find going up at auction, carpet names offer most of us no reliable indication of value. Nor do some of the often exaggerated prices that some auctioneers will quote in order to indicate what a terrific buy you might make.

It is a good—in fact, an essential—rule to bid for no carpet that you have not seen fully displayed. If an auctioneer suggests that space, time or manpower will permit him to show only half of a carpet, tell him that you regret you will be unable to bid. If he still cannot comply with your request: even if the carpet seems absolutely perfect, skip it, and keep looking until you find a carpet so exhibited that proper inspection is possible.

Expert professionals can work miracles of carpet restoration to correct certain defects. Worn spots can be rewoven, tears can be mended, crooked sides brought into some sort of alignment; curled edges can be flattened (or cut away), and frayed edges can be overcast. You could, in fact, undertake overcasting the edges, which is one of the repairs most frequently needed, yourself. All you need is a good wool yarn of the right color, a needle, a thimble, and patience. Restoration costs will vary, of course, depending on the work required. If you are going to pay $100 or more for repairs, you might want to consider applying that amount to the purchase of a carpet in better condition.

Only by seeing the rug fully exposed can you tell whether or not a portion of it has been cut away, to permit its use in a smaller room, or to eliminate some damage. If it has, the absence of a border at one side, or the abrupt termination of a design, or an obvious lack of symmetry, will alert you to the possibility that you are considering an incomplete carpet. Not only will cutting have reduced the size of the carpet; it will also have trimmed the value by half—or more. You could get many years of satisfactory use from a rug that has been cut, but you will certainly want to adjust the amount of your maximum bid to allow for its reduced worth.

Consider the thickness and the evenness of the rug's nap. Very rare antique rugs might be acceptable collectors' items in extremely thin, almost threadbare condition, for the excellent reason that they simply are not available in any other state. But those rare examples are not the badly worn carpets that you and I usually run into at auction. A slightly thin rug that is otherwise acceptable could be a good buy. If the nap is severely worn away, don't let the treasures you have seen in museums influence you to purchase a threadbare carpet. And don't think that with a little cutting and reweaving a clever restorer will make it worth a fortune. The cost will be enormous, and with rarest exceptions, the carpet will not have been worth the expenditure.

Look at the back to see whether the rug is hand-tied or machine-made. The finest handmade rugs will have been evenly knotted, but they never match machine knotting, which results in ties that are perfect as pearls, monotonously uniform, absolutely even. If you cannot recognize the difference, go to a rug dealer and ask to see examples of each. Experts say that the design of a machine-made rug looks lifelessly perfect compared with that of a handwoven carpet. As with hand-decorated porcelain as distinguished from that which is transfer-printed, once you have compared them, you should be able to tell them apart at a glance.

If sizing, or one of the nonskid backings, has been applied to the reverse, the rug is worth less—sometimes much less—than it would be without it. Sizing has probably been used to bring a poorly shaped rug into alignment, or to add needed body. Nonskid backings might be there to keep the rug from slipping—but they also can conceal serious damage.

While you are looking at the reverse, compare the color of the wool with the colors on the face. Colors on the back should be the same as, or *darker* than, the nap. Faded color on the reverse would indicate that the rug has been chemically bleached, or that the nap has been painted or dyed. It makes sense, doesn't it, that the face would fade more than the unexposed back? Treated rugs depreciate annually. A "natural" carpet, even allowing for normal wear, will usually become more valuable through the years.

Repairs that show have been made improperly and substantially reduce the value of the rug. Reduce your best offer further to allow for the cost of having the work done over.

What about new or used contemporary rugs? These show up at auction too, and some of them are sensational bargains. Certainly a fine used rug in good condition will wear longer and look better than a cheap new one, and probably can be bought for far less. Nylon is the strongest carpet fiber. If you need a rug for a heavy-traffic spot, it could be your best choice. Acrylic fibers and wool yield the next-longest-wearing rugs. Cotton wears well, but soils easily. Rayon carpets usually have the shortest lives and, consequently, would be expected to live still shorter ones if purchased in "used" condition.

A good cleaning can do wonders for a rug. Many auctioneers will refuse to sell a rug that has not been cleaned immediately before it goes on exhibition. If you do not see the cleaner's ticket on a rug, ask the auctioneer whether or not he has had the rug cleaned. If you buy a rug that has not been cleaned, you might ask the cleaner to remove the rug from the auction premises and have it cleaned before it is delivered to your home.

SILVER

Some auctioneers will cheerfully suggest that with a few light taps of a hammer, you can repair a minor dent in a piece of silver. Don't believe it! And above all, don't try it unless you have the proper tools and happen to be an experienced silversmith. It would be better to leave the piece alone than to risk greater damage as a result of your attempts to eliminate a minor flaw. The best thing you can do to improve the appearance of a beautiful piece of antique silver is polish it. Any other attention that seems to be in order should be handled by an expert. That will add to the cost of the piece, but probably will not increase its value. So you will want to adjust your maximum bid accordingly.

Most of the antique silver put up at auction in the United States is either American or English, and only about 10 percent of that will be unmarked, or illegibly marked. Certain auctioneers make a great fuss about the presence of hallmarks on British silver, but for nearly seven hundred years marking of all British silver has been required by law. It is what the marks mean that matters. With a little experience, a magnifying glass and a good reference guide, you should be able to identify the date, place of origin and maker of at least nine out of ten examples of English silver. Breathe on the hallmark, though, to see if it is original to the piece. The haze of moisture will reveal the borders of a silver inlay bearing marks that might have been lifted from a damaged piece. Markings on American antique silver tend in one way to be simpler and in another more complex, since they might consist of nothing more than the maker's initial or monogram, or occasionally may be a fully written name. You might have to consult several reference books to authenticate a particular signature. If you succeed, you at least can place the piece within the craftsman's lifetime. Researchers have documented the marks of several thousand American silversmiths—which makes identification possible, but a good deal more tedious than deciphering the marks on a British piece.

The word STERLING marks some British silver dating from the sixteenth and seventeenth centuries. This word is seldom found on American silver articles made more than one hundred years ago. Somewhat earlier American pieces are much more likely to be marked PURE COIN or WARRANTED, or both— by which designations nineteenth-century silversmiths sought to distinguish their work from the cheaper silver-plated wares then new to the American market.

Pure silver is extremely light in weight, and sterling is $925/1000$ pure. If you are trying to determine whether or not an unmarked or illegibly marked piece is sterling, test its weight. If it seems unexpectedly light, it usually will be. Silver-plated ware, on the other hand, will usually feel surprisingly heavy. Silver has a characteristic smell, too. With a bit of practice, you can probably train yourself to distinguish it from that of other silvery metals.

Although antique silver plate has become nearly as costly as sterling, contemporary plated ware frequently brings unbelievably low prices at auction. Look for signs of bleeding at the points of maximum wear—handles, finials, feet, covers—and at the high points of decoration or shape where polishing action would have been strongest. Get approximate cost estimates on replating before you buy a piece that needs it. Just because a few years ago you had a beautiful Victorian cookie basket resilvered for a song, don't assume that comparable work will be the same price tomorrow. Some auctioneers will suggest that for $5, or $6, you can have the piece looking like new. It could cost three, four, five or more times as much. And that might be more than you want to spend. You might, in fact, find that for the purchase price plus the cost of replating, you could have bought a piece of sterling silver, or a more desirable piece of plated ware in good condition. Badly tarnished silverplate is difficult to evaluate. You might be happily surprised to find that it polishes beautifully. Remember, though, that any worn spots will be even more noticeable when some of the surface shines.

There are some interesting methods for cleaning tarnished plated ware. Simmering things in soda water in a foil-lined aluminum kettle can give one a definite feeling of kinship with the ancient alchemists, and actually might do some good. Some people swear by toothpaste, although it costs more to use than regular commercial silver polish. I don't know of anything short of electroplating, however, to restore silver plating that has worn away. If you don't want to polish and don't want to replate, leave the tarnished bargains for some other buyer.

Monogrammed silver presents definite problems to some people if the monogram isn't theirs. Actually, most guests never notice such an incongruity, and if one does, he can usually be counted on not to make an issue of it. Besides, it could have belonged to your maternal grandmother, couldn't it? Well . . . If such things trouble you, consider having the old engraving removed and your own initials substituted. Keeping an open mind can certainly lead you to some astonishing auction buys.

TABLES
(Antique)

Drop-leaf tables have been popular in America since Colonial times. They saved space then, giving maximum seating from minimum storage, and they save space today. They're attractive, practical, extremely well built and, except for the sort of wear that also shortens the legs of chairs (probably because they were moved about less, tables seem to suffer somewhat less from it), are apt to be found in what will look like astonishingly good condition. Reserve your judgment until you have seen the table with *both* leaves elevated. Now, just how warped are they? Can you use the table "as is"? Can the curve be eliminated or reduced to a slight waviness that you can pass off as an optical illusion?

There are repairs that will uncurl those leaves. The most drastic, I think, involves cutting the boards apart and regluing them after patient applications of moisture and pressure. The simplest, I've been told, involves newspapers and tons of old books. (And probably a good deal of intensive prayer as well.) Again, this is a matter best left to an expert. The most important thing you can do in inspecting any drop-leaf table on which you are considering making a bid is to be sure that you do see it with the leaves raised. Look at it across the top from

each side and also from a short distance. Don't deceive yourself that your eyes are playing tricks on you. No matter how
straight those boards look when they're lowered, if you see a
curve when they're raised, it is *there*. Insisting on seeing the
table with the leaves elevated has the additional advantage of
assuring you that the table is in possession of both leaves. I've
seen drop-leaf tables with only one wing offered at auction.
Displayed against the wall, they looked perfectly complete.
Let's hope that's all the winning bidder planned to do with
his purchase.

Look for protruding nails in the tops of old country-kitchen
tables. Old handmade nails that have surfaced because the
wood around them has shrunk may be an excellent indication
of age, but they are also a nuisance if you want to do more
than look at your auction treasure. If you're considering an
extension table, ask to see it extended and make sure the
leaves are in good condition and that they fit together
smoothly. It should not become a problem in engineering to
open the table or to close it. The legs or pedestal bases on
extension tables are frequently insecure. Bear in mind that
this is something not likely to improve with use.

One of the most important features of a dining table is
that the top be high enough to permit you to pull a chair up
under it. Make sure, however, that the table doesn't have an
apron so deep that it prevents seating regardless of the height
of the table. There are a lot of fine old library tables and
work tables around. They would make wonderful dining tables,
too, except for a deep apron that prevents seating. Many
valuable old tavern tables not only have aprons to be considered, but also have stretchers connecting the legs. The
stretchers, set close to the floor, are charming—as long as you
don't trip over them or bruise your shins on them. Don't
rationalize that you will get used to them. Even if you do, not

all of your guests will. These tables frequently have a small drawer set into the apron. It provides a convenient place for storing silver—or Band-Aids.

Game tables often combine features of both extension tables and drop-leaf tables, and are subject to the same problems. Look for loose legs and difficult extensions. And warped —or missing—leaves. Don't be put off by the condition of the felt, but give attention to the veneer. You can glue on a piece of new felt quicker than I can suggest it, but either a bad chip in the veneer is going to just sit there staring at you, or else off goes your table to that reliable old restorer.

4 HOW TO ATTEND AN AUCTION

"BRING CHAIRS . . . lunch . . . cartons . . . cash!" suggests one auction announcement. "Complimentary champagne served," promises another. "Cash or certified checks only!" an auction advertisement specifies in uncompromisingly bold type. "Buffet available," another ad primly says in small italic script. "The heat's on and the food's good!" is the cheerful footnote to a country auctioneer's broadside. "Deliveryman on premises!" one auctioneer advertises. "Everything cash and carry!" another warns. "Positively no children admitted to exhibition or sale," declares a card in the door of a midtown gallery. "Absolutely no reserving of seats!" insists a sign at the entrance to a suburban auction room. "Free coffee and doughnuts served until sale time!" invites a poster near the cashier's booth at an auto-auction garage.

. What you will want to take along to an auction will obviously vary with the kind of auction you attend. An announcement that suggests you bring "chairs . . . lunch . . . cartons . . . cash!" leaves no doubt about the nature of the sale, and the absense of facilities you otherwise might have expected to find. Chances are it will turn out to be an *al fresco* affair.* In which case, in addition to the recommended items,

---

* Yes, even in the dead of winter, if the sale is being held at a private house in which no one room is large enough to accommodate the audience. When we

you will want to take boots and blankets in winter, umbrellas the year around—should the rain, or the sun, become fierce (although to use your umbrella, you will probably have to stand at the back of the audience in order not to block anyone)—and some hot or cold beverage appropriate to the season and to your luncheon menu.

Lunch is a good thing to take to any all-day sale, even if the auctioneer advises that food will be available. For one thing, if food service is supplied by the management, it is likely to be a secondary part of the operation. One or two sandwich choices, soft drinks, possibly coffee and tea, and those ubiquitous individually wrapped slices of cake, identical as tombstones and about as tasty, are par for the course under such an arrangement. Help is usually in short supply, and if the sale is interrupted for lunch, the sudden rush to the food counter invariably results in waiting lines that seem not to shorten throughout the recess. A catered buffet can involve anything from frankfurters and hamburgers to dripping, hot-sauced hero sandwiches—or, with a misplaced nod toward Epicurus, paper dishes of something like creamed chicken or *goulache hongroise,* either of the latter being nearly impossible to eat neatly with a brittle plastic toy fork.

If you attend many all-day auctions, you will quickly consume a lifetime quota of ham-and-cheese sandwiches, lukewarm hot dogs and steamed hamburgers.* The alternatives to

---

began attending auctions, we would often set out on an icy day, warmed by mutual assurances that the sale could not possibly be held outside. We quickly learned that it could. The dedicated are dauntless—the mailmen are not alone in refusing to be stayed by "Neither snow, nor rain, nor heat, nor gloom of night . . ."

   * There is certainly nothing wrong with a *good* ham-and-cheese sandwich, but good ham-and-cheese sandwiches, which should be easy to assemble given reasonably sound ingredients, by some awful alchemy become transmuted in the hands of the harassed ladies who "help out" at the auction "snack bar" into pink-cardboard-and-yellow-wax sandwiches. The kitchens at one or two auction barns that I know actually serve grilled frankfurters, but most auction franks will be

this fairly standard fare are three: (1) miss an hour of the sale while you have lunch in a—hopefully—nearby restaurant; (2) go through the day without eating, which might leave you feeling a little blinky and, possibly, with a slight headache; (3) take your lunch to the auction.

Of the available choices, (1) has the disadvantage of absenting you from the sale—which, to a serious auction buff, is sufficient to warrant its immediate rejection. If you happen to be in an unfamiliar neighborhood, an additional disadvantage is that you might find yourself traveling a considerable distance for a lunch no better than that which was available at the auction. Of course, if you happen to know that there is a "perfect little jewel of a restaurant just five minutes down the road," *and* there is a long sequence of lots on which you do not plan to bid, *and* you can leave someone (or some*thing*) behind to guarantee that you will not lose your seat, *and* you are absolutely certain that that "perfect little jewel" is open (don't *assume*; schedules are notoriously idiosyncratic, weekend closings are not uncommon, hours sometimes vary with the seasons) *and* that it will not be so crowded with other patrons drawn by the auction that you will have an uncomfortably long wait, then alternative (1) could be your best choice—but only if all those qualifications are met. Advance reservations might be a good idea; in fact, if the restaurant will accept it, you might consider placing your order at that time, provided a definite hour for the auction recess has been established.

Most auctioneers pace themselves with surprising accuracy, and will move the designated number of lots within, at most,

---

fished out of a bath of scarcely simmering water and served, perhaps one degree above tepid, within the pasty shroud of a cold roll. The hamburgers once may have known the searing heat of skillet or grill, but hours of poaching between layers of stewed onions, or in the covered chambers of a steam table, will have exhausted whatever vitality they once possessed.

thirty minutes of the announced period. If your only time indication is that the sale will be interrupted between lots 200 and 201, then you need to know the auctioneer's style sufficiently well to predict the average number of lots he can dispose of in an hour. This might be anything from forty (or fewer, although moving one lot every 1½ minutes would be awfully slow going) to one hundred or more, depending on the nature of the lots, the response of the audience, the temperament of the auctioneer and the efficiency of the crew. If you note that many large, heavy items are included in the lots, you need to allow for some time lost in handling. Even the most skillful and well-organized crew takes more time to put up and remove a heavy nine-piece dining-room set than it does to show a garnet brooch. Paintings and rugs are apt to sell quickly, although rugs require extra time for handling. Interestingly, the highly desirable lots will usually be disposed of more quickly than will less valuable items. If you want to be sure to be at your seat for a particular number that happens to be preceded by many important lots, calculate the progression of sale at fifty lots moving every thirty minutes, and then get back well ahead of your estimate. If you can speak to him before the sale, ask the auctioneer at what time he expects to reach a particular lot. Chances are that he will be right, but to avoid disappointment, anticipate his estimate by at least thirty minutes.

Many sales are conducted without intermission, and without regard to any particular sequence of lots. This would make alternative (1) an unwise choice indeed.

Not eating anything for seven or eight hours is much more liable to result in fatigue, irritability, headache and dizziness at the end of an all-day auction than in a situation in which you were physically active. Sitting quietly for hours tends to lower your blood sugar. Your energy drops sharply, leaving you less mentally alert and considerably under par in the cheerfulness department, which is reason enough to reject alternative (2). If no food—or no food that you want to eat —is available, and you have not packed a lunch, take a fresh-air break and go for a brisk walk; maybe jog a bit. The important thing is to get your circulation stirred up before you begin another three or four hours of steady sitting. Even if you habitually go without lunch, it is a good idea to have some light refreshment midway through an all-day sale. Which brings us to alternative (3).

What you will want to put in your lunch box, of course, depends on what you like to eat and on how much trouble you want to take to prepare it. I have seen couples unwrap compartmented trays holding cold chicken in tarragon jelly, elegantly garnished with miniature miracles of artichoke hearts and raw mushrooms, and I have watched with undisguised envy as they washed down those appealing tidbits with cups of cool pink wine, meanwhile continuing with their quite accomplished bidding. But I couldn't help thinking what a lot of work someone must have gone to in composing those trays with near-Japanese perfection, and that the result seemed a shade self-conscious amid all the plebeian paper-wrapped squares of auction ham-and-cheese.

Messy things—foods that crumble or drip or yield seeds, shells, peels or bones—are best avoided, especially if you are going to dine at your seat and will be faced with the choice between disposing of such inedible remains and having them haunt you throughout the rest of the sale. Apples and pears, in spite of the cores, are neat to eat and, with a good chunk of almost any but the most defiantly fragrant cheese, make a perfectly dandy lunch that requires no more preparation than washing and drying the fruit, properly wrapping the cheese, and dropping both into a plastic bag. With coffee or tea (or even better, with cold milk, or wine), you have a perfectly acceptable, easy lunch that you can eat without fork, knife or spoon, that requires no plate, and that leaves you with no garbage-disposal problem beyond dropping a napkin-wrapped fruit core into the plastic bag in which your lunch was carried. If this seems an unsatisfyingly light meal, you could add a slice or two of good, honest bread, or some nuts (shelled, *please*) and raisins. The fruit-and-cheese lunch travels well, does not require refrigeration, is easily consumed and digested, and will see you through the long hours of the sale well nourished, clear-eyed and optimistic right up to the last bang of the auctioneer's hammer.

A candy bar is a good source of quick energy, and a neatly portable snack, but besides being bad for your teeth and your diet, candy has the disadvantage of increasing thirst. Undoubtedly, there are many auction rooms that provide drinking water for their patrons. I mean with a water cooler, or a fountain right out where one can get to it without having to wander around through those catacombs that unfold behind the NO ADMITTANCE signs. Personally, I happen across very few. One can try to manage with cupped palms and water from the lavatory tap, of course, as long as the facilities include a lavatory, and the water is running and potable.

Oddly enough, although drinking water may be hard to find, the sale of soft drinks in cans or bottles is practically inescapable. If you happen to feel that a sweet-flavored soda actually satisfies your thirst, and you have coins of denominations that the machine will accept, you are home free. Otherwise, avoid candy and other notorious thirst provokers such as heavily salted or highly spiced foods. Since that category includes not only the omnipresent ham-and-cheese sandwich, the frankfurter and the usual array of condiments that are obligatory with hamburgers or hot dogs, consider taking along a vacuum bottle filled with your preferred beverage, even if you choose not to take your lunch to the auction. Being able to have something to drink without leaving your seat is a great convenience and, unless you are lucky enough to be sitting on the aisle, keeps you from having to disturb your neighbors by passing back and forth.

If the auctioneer says to bring your own chairs, by all means leave those portable chaise longues by the pool or on the terrace where they belong. For one thing, they *sit* lower than other chairs, so if you don't get them planted directly in the center of row one, you are liable to have trouble seeing. For another, the long footrest that seems so comfortable for relaxing on the patio can become absolutely numbing in the course of three or four hours of sitting. Additionally, it takes up an unfair amount of space and exposes you to being crowded and tripped over. It is convenient to have a couple of aluminum folding chairs (the kind that *are* chairs) on tap in your car. Chairs with legs formed from a continuous tubular element sit the ground better than those with four separate feet, which tend to dig in at soft spots. If you don't own a pair, maybe you can pick up a couple at auction! Having your own chairs available comes in handy at sales where the auctioneer provides seating, too, in case the crowd is too large and you arrive too late to stake a proper claim to a seat that you want. Usually you can squeeze in an extra chair or two at a side aisle, or at the back of the house. People in the audience—and some auctioneers—will object if you attempt to set up in front of the established first row.

Unless you are attending a sale at one of the plush galleries where everything—including most of the audience—comes wrapped in velvet, take a pillow to the auction with you. Wooden church pews are the only seats more uncomfortable than the chairs in most auction rooms. And seldom do you sit in church for as long as four to eight hours! A seat cushion will make the time you spend at auction a good deal more pleasant. It will also serve to mark your chair when you are away from it. A small, squarish foam-rubber pillow about

1½ inches thick seems most practical to me. The best that I have found are made to use on boats and can be bought at marine-supply stores. You don't want a pillow so large that it flops uncomfortably over the edges of your chair. Or so soft that it collapses when you sit down. The deck bench cushions that we use are durable, inexpensive and compact. We seldom fail to take them with us when we go to an auction.

Even if the announcement does not suggest it, a couple of sturdy cardboard cartons will be a wise addition to your auction-going equipment. Packing service varies from auction to auction, running the gamut from nonexistent to extraordinary and hitting all the stations in between. Generally it is a good idea to arm yourself against nonexistent, unless from experience you happen to know otherwise. Nothing is worse than having to scrounge around for newspaper and boxes when both are in short supply and you have a dozen breakable items to cart away. Most auction rooms will have *some* boxes and some kind of wrapping paper available. If you look closely, you will see it lying around someplace. Finding these things and utilizing them properly will be largely up to you. Wrapping facilities are practically unheard of at house sales and country auctions. Carrying a bundle of newspapers and a couple of strong cartons can save you a lot of difficulty. Liquor stores are a good source of suitable boxes. A carton strong enough to sustain the weight of twelve liquid-filled bottles is not likely to collapse on you. Moreover, it has probably been neatly opened along three edges only, which will make it possible for you to close it again just as neatly. Take out the cardboard honeycomb that separated the bottles and you have a nice roomy container that will be adequate for almost any glass, china or other breakables you might buy at auction.

One of the secrets of break-preventive wrapping is to use

plenty of newspaper. Not only around the item itself, but inside it, and—crumpled loosely—packed tight in between it and everything else. Throw away the rotogravure sections and any other supplements printed on heavy coated stock; what you want for this purpose is nice, wrinkly, soft old newsprint. Toss a couple of Sundays' worth of newspaper into one of your cartons and make it part of your standard auction gear.

There are auctions at which you will be given beautiful wrapping service—about one in eight, from our experience. And of that 12½ percent, three out of five take place in the city.*

If lots are delivered to you at your seat, you will need your cartons and newspaper there with you. Otherwise you would have to sit holding whatever you bought throughout the sale and, no doubt, wishing you had some safe place to set it down.

At sales where no purchases are delivered until the conclusion of the auction, you might find that the scramble for cartons and wrapping paper has left nothing suitable to your needs. At those times, there is enormous satisfaction in being able to breeze out to your car and return with a couple of nice, sturdy boxes and a sheaf of newspaper.

Take along a hank of clothesline if your auction buys will include furniture, or other items too large to travel inside your car. Plain, old-fashioned cord-type clothesline—not that new plastic spaghetti that stretches and squirms when you try to draw it taut. For ease of packing and shipping, clotheslines are sold in Siamese coils joined by a central strand. What you will want to do is open both hanks and rewind the clothesline into a ball of continuous cord. Do not cut it. Find one end, tie a knot in it and start winding. You can

---

* Moving-and-storage-company auctions usually do the best wrapping job. They have all those great cartons that they use in their regular work, and the right kind of rope, and employees who know how to handle things properly.

wind it onto a wooden core if that's the kind of person you are and you happen to have a bit of dowel or an old chair rung lying around looking useless.

If you are going to start lashing things to the roof of your car, it is a good idea to have an old rug, a heavy blanket, or a strip of carpeting to spread between car roof and auction acquisition, to keep them from damaging each other. With your less-than-$3 clothesline, such otherwise unusables can save you a substantial amount in delivery charges.

Most auctioneers work with or can recommend a truckman who will arrange to deliver your more massive purchases for you. If you have bought more lots than you can handle on your own—and this includes getting things unloaded once you have them safely home (which is something you might find much more difficult than getting the same items *onto* your car, since the auction crew can usually be prevailed upon for help at that end)—you might want to consider having them delivered. (*See Chapter 7: How to Claim Your Purchases.*)

At any auction, it is a good idea to have some cash available. Some auctioneers claim that they will accept only cash or certified checks, but even if they don't *like* to do it, most will accept your personal check, provided you can back it up with satisfactory identification. A book of traveler's checks is a handy thing to have—especially if you unexpectedly attend a weekend auction and cannot get to your bank to obtain the desired "cash or certified checks only."

Eventually you will attend a sale at which you bid in more lots than you have cash, certified checks or traveler's checks to cover.* Wait until the end of the sale to settle your

* Some auctioneers now accept certain credit cards. Others undoubtedly will adopt this popular charge system in the future. If you happen to be holding the right cards at the right sales, this could be a convenient manner of payment. The auction room, however, remains, for the most part, one of the last outposts of business conducted on a strict cash basis. In view of which, it is essential to find

account. Tell the cashier that you will be glad to give your personal check for the balance. Hold your temper—and your ground. The auctioneer may insist that you pay for what you can in the manner specified by him, and return later with cash or bank checks to pay for the remaining lots. If this is acceptable to you (and in determining if it is, consider the time and expense involved in a second trip), obtain a list of the unclaimed lots that you are to receive, with identifying descriptions and prices. Have the auctioneer write on it the date by which you must claim these items, and have him sign it. Be sure that the established date is one that you can meet comfortably.

If a second trip to claim the remainder of your purchases involves substantial inconvenience to you, select the most desirable items for which you can make acceptable payment. Tell the auctioneer that either he must agree to take your check to cover the balance of your purchases, or you will reluctantly have to relinquish them. With the auction ended, the audience dispersed, and no chance of disposing of those lots until his next sale, the auctioneer might prefer accepting your check.

He would, however, be entirely in the right if he refused to deliver *any* of the lots that you have won—including those for which you are prepared to make payment in the manner specified. Conditions of sale vary from auction to auction, but customarily among them is the statement that deposits are to be applied to *all* purchases made at the sale, and not to any one particular lot. By paying only a portion of your total bill, you technically are making only partial payment on *each* of the lots that were sold to you, even though you might want to attribute the money differently in order to cover the full

out in advance whether or not your particular charge card will be honored, and if so, whether purchases so billed are subject to any service charge, or limitation.

price of certain items. If he chooses to apply that interpretation, the auctioneer will insist that since none of your purchases has been completely paid for, he is obliged to cancel all of them.

The auctioneer may elect to waive this requirement in your case, even as he might agree to accept your personal check. The important thing to remember is that he does not *have* to do it, if his conditions of sale—which should be posted on the premises, or printed in the catalogue, or announced at the beginning of the auction—include this restriction against specific attribution of deposits.

Far from being as arbitrarily harsh and high-handed as it sounds, this provision for nonattributable deposits is a protection to the serious buyer as well as the auctioneer. Without it, capricious bidders are sometimes inclined to take every lot in which they are remotely interested, bidding in one as insurance against possibly not winning another, and then, at the close of the sale, picking and choosing which of their many purchases they will actually keep and simply refusing to pay for anything about which they have changed their minds, or for which they feel they may have overbid. To discourage this "bid now, decide later," attitude, many auctioneers require that bids be secured by deposits which are applicable to all items bid in.

At many auctions at which no advance deposits are required, runners circulating through the audience will collect partial or full payment from the successful bidder as each lot is sold. If you are not prepared to make such immediate payments in cash, ask the bookkeeper to open an account for you, and secure it with a signed blank check made out to the auctioneer. (Very few cashiers are able to resist this appealing gesture. It appears to be an unfailingly impressive tactic.) At the end of the sale, you fill in the amount of your purchases and close your account.

If you do make cash deposits throughout the sale, be sure that the runner gives you a receipt for the correct amount of each payment. If you pay the full purchase price in cash, obtain a receipt—even if the runner also delivers the item to you at that time! At country-style cash-and-carry auctions where all lots are delivered and paid for as they are removed from the auction block, the possibility of a dispute about payment is unlikely. Still, you might want a receipt as a statement of presumed authenticity, or to establish ownership. The public aspect of auction sales makes them a dubious vehicle for disposal of stolen merchandise, but if the question ever did arise, a receipt would certainly come in handy!

Don't be shy about asking for a receipt. If the runner objects, or the auctioneer complains that he cannot slow down the sale by having his man take time to write up sales slips, then ask to be put on account so that you can pay your bill at the close of the sale, at which time you *can* be issued a proper receipt.

A receipt is necessary if you want to return any of your auction purchases, too. Return? That's right. Returns come right after shills in the list of things auctioneers least enjoy talking about. Almost every auctioneer will maintain that all sales made at auction are final, that all lots are sold "as is" without guarantee as to condition, or accuracy of description. And let's face it, that is one of the fundamental rules of the game. But there are still instances in which you will feel that you have good reason to return something—and in which you will be able to, provided you have a receipt showing when you bought it, where you bought it, what you paid for it, and what it was represented to be. If, on delivery, or even sometime after delivery—although a week would seem to be a reasonable limit—you find that a purchase in some way fails to fulfill the auctioneer's description, immediately contact the auctioneer, tell him what you bought and why you want to return it, and establish a time at which you can bring it back.

An appointment is important, since many auctioneers are unable to keep any sort of regular office hours. Much of an auctioneer's work may be done on the outside, not only holding sales, but also investigating future consignments. A sale lasting a few hours can represent months of negotiation and preparation. If your man is not instantly available, don't immediately assume that he is trying to avoid you. If you cannot reach him by telephone, send him a letter asking that he contact you.

Whatever you do, don't mistakenly think it would be a clever tactic to descend upon him when he is about to begin an auction. Even the most honest, patient and gracious of gentlemen is apt to respond negatively to that kind of high-pressure, eleventh-hour entrapment. Men who have been conducting auctions for many years report that before every sale they experience the kind of opening-night nerves that are a theatrical tradition.

It would be somewhat better to approach him after a sale. The problem then, however, is that tension might have been replaced by exhaustion. I have seen one auctioneer given oxygen the instant he stepped down from the platform. I have watched another, his clothes soaked through with perspiration, sit facing the wall and pressing his forehead against the cool plaster, although minutes before, he had been a hearty, cheering goad to a large and responsive crowd. The whiskey that is poured behind the scenes at the conclusion of many auctions is frequently more therapeutic than festive. Auctioneers who don't drink use smelling salts, cold towels, hot orange juice, tea laced with incredible amounts of honey —whatever they have found helps combat the letdown that comes at the end of the sale. If you absolutely must speak to the auctioneer then, be specific and brief. See if you can make an appointment for some more convenient time. Of course, there is always the possibility that he will go along with any reasonable request just to be rid of you. You really have to play it by ear.

Don't discuss your problem with the bookkeeper or any of the other workers. The auctioneer is the only one with the authority to help you. If 99 percent of the staff agrees with you and the auctioneer does not, *his* is the opinion that will usually prevail. An exception would be if the cashier, as she sometimes does, happens also to be Mrs. Auctioneer and strongly supports your case.

If the auctioneer suggests that he cannot permit you to return your purchase but will be glad to resell it for you, tell him that you would much prefer to have your payment refunded. Assuming that you have a valid reason for wanting to return the item, you do not want to risk sustaining a loss if the lot fails to bring as much as you paid. If it is included in the next sale, many potential bidders will remember having seen it. And if no one was willing to give an advance on your winning bid, it is unlikely that anyone will exceed it on a repeat offering, particularly if the auctioneer feels obliged to explain why he is reselling the lot. Returned items will occasionally bring substantially higher prices when they are resold —almost anything *can* happen at auction. If you enjoy taking bold risks, and are willing to suffer a loss, you might want to go along with the auctioneer's suggestion. Find out first, however, whether or not you will be charged a commission on the sale, and how it will be calculated. A fair arrangement would be that the auctioneer will resell the piece without charge up to the amount you paid and that if he should achieve an advance beyond that, you will pay his regular commission on the difference.

Should you come up against an obdurate type who refuses to consider a refund on a lot that you are disinclined to have him resell for you, it may be necessary for you to secure the services of an appraiser and an attorney. Before embarking on this exciting course of action, however, consider whether you will wind up paying more in appraisal and legal fees than you could possibly recover by redeeming your purchase. Add to the obvious costs the demands that will be made on your time and emotions. It might well not be worth it.

A final observation on the unpleasant matter of returns. As much as the auctioneer hates them, most buyers hate them even more. We don't like to admit that we made a mistake. That we overpaid for something worth far less than we thought. That we were taken in (if we were, maybe the auctioneer also was) by a fake signature. That we failed to notice the crack, the repair, the missing element. Many times, we would rather write the loss off to experience and tell ourselves that it was worth it, because next time we will be more cautious.

The first time I had occasion to return an auction purchase, I went through every possible rationalization against doing so before I finally realized the actual reason for my reluctance: that I was sure the auctioneer would be unpleasant about it. As it turned out, the auctioneer—although obviously not overjoyed—was eminently agreeable and gave me a full refund on the item. That my receipt showed I was returning only one of ten lots purchased did my cause absolutely no harm. Neither did the fact that I did not begin by accusing the auctioneer of having deliberately misrepresented the value of the lot. "I'm afraid we were both wrong about this one," I said, suggesting that he had presented the item with the same good faith in which I had bid for it.

I don't think it is worth the time and effort that it takes to return just any little purchase for any old reason. But if a lot is described as bronze, and you bid accordingly, I think you should expect to be given a refund if your purchase turns out to be something else that has been "bronzed." If a lot is said to be perfect, or mint, or in working order, or sterling, or marked, or signed, or anything else that would substantially increase its value or utility, and you find it to be other than as represented, don't be intimidated by the "all sales final." There is a good chance that you will be allowed to return it, provided you are not too proud to admit that you too might have made a mistake, and as long as you have obtained—and retained—a receipt.

What you will wear to the auction, like practically everything else, will depend on the auction that you are attending. There are black-tie auctions at which 85 percent of the audience shows up in evening clothes. But like opening night at the opera, these gala affairs are not events with which most of us mere mortals clutter up our social calendars. If you are invited to one, what you will wear is pretty much decreed by your host, which might be one of the more prestigious galleries in your vicinity. But even then, auctions being more-or-less public events, it is a good idea not to flash about in your finest.

We know one auction buff who enjoyed nothing more than to be adorned in some of her most glittering treasures whenever she went out to bid for more. One night, having acquired several worthwhile baubles by raising her diamond-and-emerald-sparkled fingers, she was followed from the auction by a couple of unscrupulous but observant characters who relieved her of her gems, including those for which she had had no opportunity to obtain insurance. While she has not taken to getting herself up like Apple Annie, the lady has since been attending auctions in something less than her "best." She has found, she tells us, that from those auctioneers to whom she is known only by number, she now makes substantially better buys than she did when sporting her more spectacular finery. In short—there are advantages in not looking too outrageously prosperous when you go to buy at auction, and they are not concerned exclusively with thieves.

If you are going to end the day roping an armoire to the roof of your car, you'll be glad that you saved your gladdest rags for some more suitable occasion. Of course, if on the other hand you show up looking too seedy, you have only yourself to blame if the auctioneer winces when you ask him to accept your check.

Be sure you wear something that you can sit comfortably in for several hours. And shoes that won't let you down if you have to stand, or go hiking across several fields to get from your car to an auction barn.

At any outdoor auction, it is a good idea to have something to cover your head and your arms. Even—or perhaps, especially—if it is a hot, sunny day.

The tiniest minority of auction rooms that we have found are air-conditioned. Practically all of them, on the other hand, are almost tropically overheated in winter. After a while, you begin to wonder if all auctioneers grow orchids behind the scenes. The requirements for a suitable auction site—adequate seating for a substantial crowd, room for storage and display, accessibility for delivery and dispatch of large consignments of heavy merchandise—tend to rule out most recent constructions. Additionally, I think many auctioneers feel that a certain degree of quaint discomfort actually enhances the appeal of their sales.

I asked the manager of a suburban gallery why he didn't install air conditioning so that he could hold sales throughout the summer instead of taking his chances on the weather and occasional hit-or-miss outdoor auctions. "Well," he said, "if I make the gallery too comfortable, they'll come to me instead of buying tickets for the movie across the street. We have enough seats going to spectators as it is. They come for the fun. It's free, and I guess we put on a pretty fair show. If

I made it more comfortable, I'd have to stretch the walls, and the real buyers would get crowded out by the onlookers. The good customers, the regulars, would sit through the flames of hell anyway, if there was something they wanted going up for sale. Besides, if I got too fancy, the place wouldn't be the same. First thing you know, I'd have to start wearing a jacket. The establishment would lose character. People like the place to be a little primitive. Makes it seem more like they're getting some real buys. You make it too fancy, they get scared off. Figure everything would bring top dollar in a place like that."

You can adapt that thinking to your appearance at auction. If you look like a millionaire, be prepared to pay "top dollar" for anything you really want. Since the auction itself is something of a staged event—a certain amount of theatricality being involved in the presentation of merchandise, in establishing the sequence of lots, in the conduct of the sale—you might as well assign a favorable role to yourself and dress the part as carefully as an actor selects his wardrobe. Sensible—perhaps a touch conservative, even if your personal taste tends toward exotica—and neither too plush nor too poor: that's the look that's "in" with successful auction buyers, season after season. What you don't want to do is stand out in the crowd. Don't worry that the auctioneer won't notice you. Bid effectively, and he will! There's no special value in being noticed by anyone else.

Winning many bids can make you something of a target for less successful competitors. Your number or the initials under which you are running an account afford you at least a veil of anonymity. That, however, is easily compromised by any outstanding bit of costuming by which you can be identified. And it stays with you throughout the sale, even if you change seats, move to the back of the room, or ask the bookkeeper to give you a different number or other initials.

There is an old, seldom-invoked auction convention that in the event of a tie bid, the bidder sitting closest to the auctioneer is considered to be the winner. It is doubtful that you will attend many auctions where this tradition is known, much less observed. On the other hand, it lends at least a historical reason for electing to sit down front. Certainly the front seats at auction are invariably the most sought-after.

There are only two ways of guaranteeing yourself a seat in the first two or three rows. And only one of them is fail-safe. That is to arrive early enough to be able to have your choice of seats or of locations in which to place your own chair. The other, somewhat less reliable, way, if chairs are provided by the management, is to telephone ahead—or write, if there is time—and ask to have a front seat reserved for you. Some auctioneers will do this, particularly if you are traveling an hour or two in order to attend their sales. Other auctioneers will promise to hold seats even though they sometimes do not. Or they might establish reservations, but fail to enforce them if someone else happens to claim the seat. Occasionally you can guarantee a reserved seat by obtaining a bidding number and securing it with an advance deposit. At certain sales, you may be *required* to obtain a bidding number in order to be assigned a seat. The glamour galleries issue jealously sought invitations or tickets of admission to their major sales at which a choice seat in the main room carries incredible cachet. Most often, however, if you want to sit close to the auctioneer, even though it might never win you a decision in a tie bid, the best way to manage it is to arrive early.

How early? Would you believe at least an hour before the start of the sale? And in many, many instances, as much as two hours? That is, *if* you want to be sure that you have a seat up front.

What do you do for two hours while waiting for the auction to begin?

(1) Claim your chair. Put your cushion on it and, if necessary, your name. Need something to write on? Tear a page out of your notebook. Ask the bookkeeper for a bit of tape. If she doesn't have any, try a Band-Aid, or one of the adhesive stickers used to number lots. Or write your name on a corded shipping tag and make it part of your regular auction "take along." If you don't want to be identified by name, just print RESERVED on the tag. If you write it importantly—big letters, black marking pen—it will probably be honored. (People pay attention to any sign that looks sufficiently definite.)

Some people think that their bidding numbers are ideal to use for marking their chairs, but that is a serious mistake. If bidding numbers are assigned, your number is your identification for that sale, and any lot knocked down to that number will be charged to your account. At a sale where lots move directly from the auction block to the successful bidder, anyone who happened to pick up your number might be able to buy against it, accept delivery of the lots, and walk out, leaving you responsible for his purchases. The auctioneer's recollection that you had been buying with that number might tend to protect you, assuming you had bid in a few lots before someone else found your number. On the other hand, the auctioneer has no way of knowing whether or not the person bidding with your number is doing so on your authority, since it is not unusual for several members of a party to use a single number. If you have not made any purchases and have secured your number with a deposit, anyone who found your number could reclaim your deposit by returning the number to the cashier. If your purchases had not exceeded the amount of your advance deposit, anyone holding your number could obtain a PAID slip, pocket any remaining difference, and take delivery of the items that you won. Conversely, if your purchases exceeded the value of your deposit, anyone holding your number could, by paying the difference, obtain delivery of the things that you bought. Whether or not it represents a cash deposit, keep your bidding number with you at all times throughout the sale. If the number is given to you in some permanent form—such as a wooden paddle—return it *to the bookkeeper* when you leave the sale. If, as it often will be, the number is an expendable piece of cardboard, obviously intended for use only at that sale, and you have not given it to the cashier in order to reclaim your deposit or to have your bill prepared, either destroy the number, if you leave while the sale is in progress, or take it with you.

(2) Obtain your bidding number, if numbers are being used. Give your deposit, if one is required. Obtain a receipt. If the cashier says that your number will be sufficient to serve as your receipt, see if you can pay your deposit by check. If cash is required, and no separate receipt is offered, have the amount of your deposit written on your numbered card and have the cashier sign it to acknowledge payment. Do not be so rushed, or so sensitive, that you fail to do this. Do not be intimidated if the cashier says that no one else ever asks her to do anything like that. Be pleasantly firm and suggest that much as you hate being such a bother, you really must insist on some sort of record of your cash deposit. A piece of cardboard with a bidding number on it is *not* sufficient, if for no other reason than that it undoubtedly is far from unique. Don't be reassured by phrases like "But nobody would do that *here!*" Probably that is entirely true. Just the same, if you are going to pay cash in advance, you have a right to expect written acknowledgment of the payment, even if it is nothing more official than the cashier's notation on a corner of your bidding number. If the sale is going to be cash-and-carry and you wish to establish a bidding account, that is something else to do.

(3) Complete your inspection, if the exhibition is still being held.

(4) Study the catalogue. Make sure your list is in order. Make any last-minute revisions on your bids.

(5) Read the Conditions of Sale, which, if not printed in the catalogue, ought to be posted in the auction room.

(6) Find out if you can settle your account and claim your purchases at any time during the sale, or if you will have to wait until all the lots have been disposed of. Make sure that if you do not make any purchases, you can reclaim your deposit at any time during the sale. Invariably you can, but it always is wise to be on the safe side.

(7) Locate the toilet.

(8) Check on food and beverage service. And drinking water.

(9) Investigate packing facilities. If you will need a carton, this is a better time to claim it than after the sale, when everyone will want a carton.

(10) Observe the crowd. If inspection continues until sale time, notice who is giving special attention to the lots on which you are planning to bid.

(11) Discuss the sale with your neighbors. Give no indication what you plan to buy, but listen and learn. If you are not acquainted with the auctioneer, see if you can't find out something about the way he conducts the sale.

(12) Miscellaneous: Drink coffee; work crossword puzzles; knit; do needlepoint; write a letter to someone you would not write to if you didn't have a few spare minutes; read—whatever you like *except* any of the various antiques price books.*

---

* These valuable publications are great to have at your elbow when you are establishing your maximum bids, and for postexhibition research; but in the auction room, they can tempt you to careless bidding and—especially if the auctioneer is less than meticulous about the accuracy of his descriptions—costly mistakes. The prices given in the guidebooks are for genuine antiques. Reproductions frequently look exactly like the pieces illustrated. In fact, recent fabrications are such excellent copies that careful examination is necessary to identify them. Seeing a lot sold for perhaps one-tenth its book value can tempt you to bid for something you have not inspected. If the article is genuine, it will prob-

Some of these activities, naturally, will require more time than others. If you allow an average of ten minutes for each, your two-hour wait will breeze past. Of course, if the hours of inspection are those immediately before the sale, you will want to devote most of your time to that. After all, you can probably drink coffee while the sale is in progress. (Especially if you brought your thermos, right?)

With lunch, if the hours of auction recommend it; chairs, if they are needed; pillows, unless you know in advance that the seats are upholstered; a couple of sturdy cartons, unless you are sure that your purchases will be well wrapped; a bundle of newspapers, ditto; a length of clothesline and a blanket, should you have to transport something bulky; enough cash to cover any deposits you might have to make; certified checks or traveler's checks, unless you know your personal check will not be refused—you will probably feel as if you are equipped to set forth in search of the lost continent of Atlantis. Nothing very terrible will happen if you eliminate or forget one or two things on the list. Ingenuity can solve many an auction problem. If you don't have cartons and newspaper, you always can wrap breakables in a blanket, or in toilet tissue, or paper towels. Sometimes the auction lots can supply what you need. It is not unusual to see someone without a seat bid in a chair at a dollar or two, use it throughout the sale, and then resell it to the auctioneer or to someone

---

ably prove to be damaged. If it is new, you will probably have overpaid. Use those reliable price books at exhibition, use them when preparing your auction list, but leave them at home when you attend a sale.

It is unwise for another reason also to take such reference books to your seat: they mark you as something of a tyro, which can tempt the auctioneer to run your bids. I have seen whole rows of people sitting at auction and concentratedly turning the pages of their price books with the precision of the violin section of a symphony orchestra working its way through a score. They frequently make a lot of buys—often to their subsequent disappointment. We use these reference books almost continuously, but we make it a rule never to take them into the auction room when it's sale time.

in the audience, or discard it. The same applies to pillows. Bundles of household linens, yard goods, fabric swatches, old rugs or scraps of carpeting can usually be bought inexpensively and make satisfactory, if somewhat odd, wrappings for more important purchases. Laundry, fruit and kindling baskets are usually inexpensive and can substitute for cartons. The one thing you cannot substitute for, or improvise at the last minute, is your auction list.

How you list the lots on which you want to bid is a matter of personal preference. If a catalogue of the auction has been published, you have the advantage of a complete list of lots in sequence of sale. On the basis of your exhibition notations, you might want nothing more detailed than a marginal indication of the amount of your maximum bid. This kind of list is most satisfactory if the catalogue entries are well spaced, or if there are only a few scattered lots in which you are interested. If the "catalogue" is one of those single-spaced jobs—as many of them are—with lot numbers following in almost unreadable sequence, and entries carried in double columns, you might find it more practical to prepare a separate list. Particularly if you want to indicate bids for many items. Whichever you do, write it in ink, for the same practical reasons for which you used ink for your inspection notes.

Don't expect that you will instantly remember every qualifying detail of each lot. To one degree or another, everyone gets caught up in the excitement of an auction. Your maximum offer might seem shockingly unrealistic in light of the competitive bidding. On the other hand, your rivals might not have noticed the defect that you took into consideration in establishing your highest bid. You will be less tempted to exceed that figure if a glance at your auction list reminds you that the item is damaged, incomplete or whatever. The notebook that you used at the exhibition is convenient for preparing your list. Except that the lots may not appear in proper numerical sequence—the exhibition having been mounted for effective display rather than order of lots—your inspection notes could do double duty as your auction list. If the lots are impossibly jumbled, it would be worthwhile to rewrite them.

In preparing your list, skip at least two lines after each entry. If space permits, make it four or five lines. Why? So that you will be able to make any late additions without disturbing the numerical order of your list. Frequently, you will spot an item that escaped your notice at the exhibition. Sometimes additional lots are included at the last minute. And, of course, you may find yourself unexpectedly bidding on an item you neglected to include on your original list. (Such as that sudden, irresistible bargain that you didn't think you could possibly win!) Having your purchases arranged in numerical sequence is a convenience when you are ready to settle your account. In addition, by integrating impulse buys into your list of planned purchases, you can quickly determine how much you have actually committed yourself to pay, and how much more you had possibly planned to spend. Having this kind of information at your fingertips is a reliable antidote for auction fever, and discourages getting carried away by the heat of competition.

Dissatisfaction with auction buys most often results from two easily avoided errors: bidding on uninspected lots, and bidding substantially beyond a previously determined maximum sum. All of us do both at one time or another—occasionally to our benefit, but far more often with the kind of sinking awareness that we have ourselves to blame for an impulsively purchased white elephant.

"Know enough to quit," urges Louis Liebson of the Astor Galleries in New York. "Pack in in time, and don't let yourself get drawn into a competitive situation in which you are determined, regardless of the cost, not to lose out to a particular rival. If something you planned to buy passes the bid at which you wanted to take it—let it go," recommends Mr. Liebson, who has been conducting auctions since 1935.

Having determined for which lots you want to bid, and how far you wish to bid, you have only to decide in what manner you can most effectively place your offer. Advances in transportation and communications have made it possible to buy at auctions in other cities, and even in foreign countries. Galleries with offices in several cities will frequently arrange for bids to be given via special telephone or television facilities connecting salesrooms from coast to coast, making it possible for bidders in Los Angeles, or Houston, to compete for lots being sold in New York. Order bids can be registered with the American representatives of several of Europe's major auction houses, and satellite communication will undoubtedly make the transatlantic auction increasingly popular. In such instances, most bidders will have to rely on catalogue information and gallery estimates* in order to decide on a maximum offer. Estimates, however, are sometimes wildly inaccurate, and might best be used as a guide to the relative values of lots in the sale. On a dozen lots in a recent London auction, a friend of mine gave the New York office order bids of £50 beyond each estimate, and was successful in only one bid.

Assuming that you are present in the salesroom, should you leap enthusiastically forward, giving the auctioneer his opening demand and hoping, by display of enthusiasm, to discourage potential rivals, or should you quietly sit back, letting the bid run what appears to be its course, and then move in for the kill with a last-minute show of beautifully calculated sangfroid? Devotees of the latter system are fun to watch in operation, but difficult for most of us to emulate. So are all those covert bids—little nods and winks, casual tugs of the

* Important lots sometimes are exhibited at more than one location.

earlobe, folding of arms, crossing of legs, buttoning or un-buttoning of coats, half-turns to the right, quarter-turns to the left, putting on and taking off of glasses—that make such fascinating reading in the accounts of important auctions.

One well-known antiques dealer with whom I have attended many sales habitually stands close beside the auctioneer and bids by giving a quick pull at the back of the man's jacket. If the auctioneer fails to acknowledge a gentle tug by giving the dealer the next advance, a firm prod with the forefinger, or even a determined pinch, might signal the following bid. Poker-faced throughout, the dealer buys anonymously, while the auctioneer, with only an occasional wince or twitch of response, goes along with the tactics in order to appease an important customer. There are certain auctions—usually small and concerned with a single commodity—at which a majority of the interested bidders are able to cluster around the auctioneer, pulling and tugging, prodding and pinching as increases are called. No one appears to be bidding, but the auctioneer evidently knows that a tug at his right sleeve is an offer from Mr. S., while a jab in the left side represents an advance from Mr. Y.

Some dealers seek anonymity by bidding from corridors adjacent to the salesroom, or from semi-concealed positions where draperies or large furniture lots shield them from the audience. These buyers are usually well known to the auctioneer or the bid callers, and can afford to risk bidding from an obscure place where less familiar offers might be ignored. With uncanny accuracy, most auctioneers can predict the lots for which their regular buyers will make an offer. They know exactly where to look for the most likely bid. Another member of the audience not only might not be recognized if he tried to bid from such a location, he might not even be allowed to occupy it.

Especially if the auctioneer does not know you, it is best to forget all those glamorous covert bids and openly indicate your interest. Leave the obscure signals to the agents of movie stars, millionaires and museums. If you don't want your wife or second cousin or archrival to know that you are bidding for a particular lot, you can always move to the back of the crowd and bid vigorously from there. Otherwise, you risk getting your signals confused or misinterpreted; you might think you have bid in a lot that is knocked down to someone whose technique is a little less subtle than yours. Especially when you are entering your first bid for a lot, be certain that the auctioneer recognizes you. Once he has, you should not have to worry that he will fail to come back to you as the bid continues.

The most common way to make a bid is to raise your hand. If you have been given a paddle, or a bidding number, hold that up. If not, hold up your catalogue, or your notebook. The auctioneers will see your bid much more readily. If you are in a disadvantageous position and feel that the auctioneer cannot see your bid, call it out, either repeating the amount, or saying "Here," or simply, "Bid."

But when to bid? Ay, there's the rub. There are sales at which all interested bidders raise their paddles the moment the lot is opened. The auctioneer begins calling bids and, as various levels are reached, those bidders who do not wish to continue lower their paddles until all but one have been eliminated, at which point the lot is knocked down to him. Lots usually move quickly at such sales, and a neophyte might find the bidding difficult to follow. At any auction it is important to know in advance for which lots one wants to bid, and what would be the maximum offer for each, but at sales where bids are taken in this manner, it is essential.

When you should bid really depends on your disposition, the auctioneer's conduct and the competition you are bidding against. If you aren't expert at the kind of cool detachment that will enable you to show casual unconcern while others contend for something that you want, don't expect to use the late-bid technique with any notable success. There's nothing terribly wrong with bidding first, you know. In fact, some auctioneers privately admit that they are inclined to favor the initial bidder and will give preference his way in the event of a dispute.

The early bid has the following disadvantages: (1) it may encourage others to bid against you by suggesting that the lot has some value that they failed to notice; (2) it could encourage an auctioneer to run your bid, if he feels that you are determined to have the lot at any price; (3) if the conditions of the sale require that a lot will not be sold unless it has drawn a minimum of two or more bids, the first offer cannot possibly succeed.

(1) applies principally to dealers, recognized collectors and celebrities, which, unquestionably, most of us are not. Of course, if you go around telling everyone about the fantastic finds you make at auction, you will acquire a certain limited celebrity that eventually will inspire others to bid against you. (2) is best corrected by a bit of carefully applied strategy that will be detailed in *Chapter 6: How to Avoid Bidding Against Yourself*. (3) is a matter of policy with some auctioneers, or is introduced at certain sales, or to protect the price of certain lots within a sale. If three bids are required, there's nothing wrong with making yours the first, since you could then offer the third—and possibly final—bid. If you know that the auctioneer's required minimum is two bids, there's very little point in favoring him with the first, except that you do risk losing the lot by having no one bid for it. Should that happen, however, console yourself with the realization that if no one else was interested enough to bid for the item, it would not have gone to you if you had given the first offer, since there

would have been no second bid for you to top.* Some auctioneers will allow you to enter a bid in advance of your own.
Others operating under the two-bid minimum will insist that
there be genuine competition for any lot to be sold, and will
not take the second offer from the original bidder.

If you are going to bid first, should you give any opening
the auctioneer demands? Again, that depends. On the auctioneer, this time. Some men will accept any first offer given,
and let the bidding advance from there. Others will ask
double or triple the amount at which they actually expect the
lot to open, feeling that this enhances the apparent value of
the offering. I know one auctioneer whose first-requested
figure invariably is within a few dollars of the final bid. He
works his way down through a long preamble of descending
amounts. Finally someone enters a bid, and then back up the
auctioneer goes, until a graph of the bids called on any lot
would describe a perfect V, with the actual opening bid as its
nadir. A number of auctioneers say that they *like* to start a lot
with a low offer, in order to encourage wider participation in
the bidding. "If I can get five or six people emotionally involved, I know that I will sell at a better price than if I open
so high that all but one or two buyers are closed out," one
auctioneer claims.

Some buyers, while perfectly willing to enter the first bid,
habitually offer half the requested start. And some auctioneers
will accept it, usually adding, "All right, let's see where it
goes," or, "I don't care where it starts, where it stops is what

* There is, of course, the possibility that the auctioneer will throw in a bid
against you. If he does that on the second bid, he will probably also do it on the
fourth, or the sixth, or the eighteenth, until he has achieved what he considers
to be a satisfactory offer. In which case there is no merit in lamenting the
bargain that you might have had on the third bid—or the fifth, or the seventh,
or the nineteenth, for that matter. You haven't lost a thing. Be suspicious of sales
at which many lots fail to draw the required number of bids.

hurts!" Others, feeling that a reduced offer might have an adverse effect on the bidding, will cry, "Refused!" and restate the original demand. Many auctioneers will insist on opening important lots at their first-requested figure, but will accept reduced bids to start routine items. And let's face it, if you know that a lot can be expected to bring something in the neighborhood of $500, you are going to look pretty silly if you insist on trying to start it off at $5.

This has nothing to do with bidding in a lot that you feel has greater worth than the auctioneer, or your competitors, may realize. If it is apparent from the requested opening that the auctioneer has undervalued a lot, it may be that he actually plans to obtain it for himself, either for inclusion in a more important sale or for resale privately, and is trying to discourage bidding. On the other hand, he or his cataloguer might have made an inaccurate appraisal, and you could be on your way to a worthwhile find. In which case, you would be well advised to (1) bid first, but with no evident enthusiasm, rather as if you felt you were doing the auctioneer a favor by taking the lot off his hands; (2) offer half—or less—of the amount of the auctioneer's already low original demand. It is quite possible that you will be able to take the lot on that one bid.*

If someone enters a bid against yours, don't rush forward with the next advance. If the auctioneer knocks down the lot to your competitor before allowing anyone a chance to continue the bidding, you can feel that you have lost nothing, because at any reasonable price the lot would have gone to

---

* In this way, I once bought an exquisite piece of eighteenth-century cream-ware for $1. Heaven knows what the auctioneer thought it was, or how he happened to have it, but he described it only as "an old dish" (which it certainly is) and asked for a start of $5. When no one responded, he asked for $2.50, and in the silence that followed, I suggested $1. Pleased to have realized anything on the "old dish," the auctioneer knocked it down to me. It isn't a particularly valuable piece, but it gives me a lot of pleasure, some of which stems from remembering the auction at which I acquired it.

your rival, who apparently was buying for the house. Otherwise, you will have a chance to offer another advance before the lot is sold. It is possible that your competitor shares your awareness of the value of the lot, and will bid right along with you until something close to its actual worth is realized. But it is equally possible that the second party entered the bidding simply because the amount was low, and will not continue beyond his initial bid.

There are people who habitually bid once on anything that seems to be going cheap, or because the item is blue, or for any of countless unfathomable reasons—including, no doubt, a feeling that they attain some special status simply by making many bids.* It is astonishing how few lots they actually win, considering the number of bids they give. On impulse they will offer a few dollars on almost anything, but they seldom constitute serious competition to an informed buyer, and can usually be expected to retire after a single low bid. It is, however, precisely these capricious types that you want to emulate when trying to bid in a lot that you feel has been undervalued. Even if the auctioneer knows you to be an astute buyer, let him think that you have occasional moments of impulsive weakness in which you might bid on something of no special merit. The better you can carry off the role, the better are your chances of making an occasional steal.

If you know that the auctioneer will not open the bidding on a lot at less than his first demand, and if that figure is at least three bids under your established maximum offer, you might as well give it to him.

---

* This is not entirely untrue. It is possible to become quite well known at auction without ever actually making a purchase. Some such people, of course, make a kind of "nuisance" or "nut" reputation for themselves. Others become recognized as canny or crafty simply because of their persistent underbidding. For my money, the smart bidder is the one who takes home what he wants, at his price. Unless they are given as part of some bidding strategy, all those other gestures are either meaningless or mistakes.

How can you tell what would equal three bids? You have to judge by the opening bid, and your knowledge of each auctioneer's method. Some men will take $10 advances all the way, even if a lot opens at $250. Custom varies, but on the average, most auctioneers will ask increments of $1 on lots opening at less than $10. On a lot starting between $10 and $25, an average increase would be $2.50. A $5 increase might most often be asked after an opening between $25 and $50, although in many cases an auctioneer will insist on $10 bids after starting a lot at $30 or $40. Certainly $10 advances would be expected on any lot opening at $50 to $100, with $25 considered by many to be an appropriate increase in that area. After $100, the auctioneer might go by increases of $25, $50 or even $100. In the last instance, he will usually announce that bids will be taken at $100 increments. At $500, he might take $50 bids, and again would probably give advance notice if he planned to move forward by $100. That $100 amount would be a minimum increase on a lot opening at $1,000, with larger bidding units specified in advance.

Except for voice bids—about which more later—opening bids, and late bids when a lot is about to close and a smaller advance might be accepted, it is wise to let the auctioneer set the amount at which bids are taken. Otherwise, an attempt to reduce the bid will usually fail. It wastes time and can be confusing, embarrassing and antagonizing. Avoid it. If the auctioneer cannot get his requested advance, and he does not himself reduce the bid, he probably would not have accepted a lower advance from you.

There are sales at which every lot opens at the amount set by the auctioneer. Prices at those auctions invariably run high. This does not mean that you cannot buy successfully at such sales. You can. Only don't expect to steal anything. And if you feel that you are going to have to bid your best price in order to take a lot, you might be inclined to hold back until the bid has come near that level before you enter the fray.

The principal disadvantage of waiting until the bid is about to close before making your first offer is that the entrance of a new bidder sometimes gives fresh life to the competition. It is quite possible that your strategic last-minute knockout bid will rekindle flagging bidding interest, and carry the lot far beyond the price at which you had hoped to take it. "Now we have a new bidder!" the auctioneer will enthusiastically announce, and all of a sudden, the bidding, which had seemed to have run its course, acquires an exciting new dimension. The two bidders who had gone down to the wire with the lot may be more than ever determined not to lose it. Someone who had retired during the early bidding might decide to get back into it. Suddenly everything looks different. What had threatened to become a weary stalemate has the bright, dynamic aspect of a fresh contest. Even those not directly involved in the bidding sense the new current of excitement in the audience.

The auctioneer beams. He knows what is probably going to happen. Suddenly four people are involved in the bidding. And someone else decides that if the others are all that desperate to have the lot, it must be something worth taking, and that he had better have a go at it. All of this is happening, mind you, when the lot has about reached its top price. You offer the next advance, which takes you one bid over your maximum. Each of your now-four competitors makes another advance. Your next bid would be six bids higher than your established limit. And if you don't take it, there are three now-eager bidders who will! It would appear that your plan to come in late for the kill had backfired pretty severely.

It would probably have been more successful if you had made your initial move while the bidding was still three or four bids under your preferred maximum—assuming, of course, that you have set a realistic rather than a ridiculous limit for yourself. This would have given you a bit of working margin to use while the competition went through the motions of getting in its last licks, and would afford some protection against the kind of flurry that can follow the emergence of a new bidder late in the game.

A bit of late strategy that can sometimes bring the bidding to a sudden close is to jump one or two bids in your initial offer. This tactic might discourage those who had previously retired from the bidding from coming back in against you, and it can shock the two remaining bidders into abrupt withdrawal. You may feel, if you take the lot with that bid, that you have gone two or three bids more that you would have had to, but by making such a dramatic entrance, you may actually have saved yourself several bids. You also risk having suggested to the auctioneer that you would make a superb target for a bit of running; but having held the lot on the block while the bidding ran its course, and having received a double or triple advance with your jump bid, he may feel it prudent not to be too greedy, and move swiftly on to the next item.*

The late bid simply cannot work every time, and probably is most effective if reserved for the one or two important lots on which you plan to bid highest. A certain unpredictability in the way you bid can work to your advantage. For one thing, it makes it harder for the auctioneer and the competition to anticipate your moves. It discourages someone in the audience from bidding you up out of spite—that *does* happen, most often after you have successfully bid against him. And

---

* Having done this, you must be alert that you do not become a target for running on later lots in which you are interested. One way to discourage it: make one or two low, early bids on a following lot that you do not want to win, and retire quickly. Give the auctioneer a good, negative signal as you refuse the next advance, as if you regret having lost whatever-it-is. The whole purpose is to establish yourself as someone who will not bid beyond a predetermined figure no matter how much he might want a particular lot. A little image-making can pay off in the auction room too, you know.

it discourages the auctioneer from playing games with you, if he happens to be the game-playing type. Adopt a chameleon style, and color your bidding strategy according to the caliber of the lot. Bid early for inexpensive items, late for those that will be more costly. And don't be afraid to lose a few bids at every sale. There are businessmen who borrow money that they really do not need, simply to establish themselves as good credit risks against the time when they might want a loan. By letting yourself lose an occasional lot, you establish yourself as someone not susceptible to running, against the time when your eagerness to win a bid might make you vulnerable to it.

We have been proceeding on the assumption that you're sitting where the auctioneer can clearly see your bids. That was your reason for arriving two hours early—to establish yourself in a front seat. But you can't always be two hours early. Or even one hour. In which case—unless your advance request for a reserved seat was honored and enforced—you are probably not sitting in front. The question then is where *not* to be sitting.

Obviously, try not to sit behind, beside, or directly in front of columns, posts, poles or other obstructions. Seated behind one, you probably can't see and undoubtedly can't be seen. Sitting pressed up against one side, or the front, is liable to be pretty confining after an hour or two, even if it doesn't seem too uncomfortable at first. Additionally, your view is partially obstructed, and if you want to turn around to see who bid against you (rude, perhaps, but occasionally desirable), you might not be able to.

The two criteria for a good auction seat are that you can see the lots as they are displayed on the block, and that the auctioneer can see you. And don't assume that because you can see *him*, it necessarily follows that he can see *you*. In many auction rooms there are areas outside the immediate range of the auctioneer's vision. Occasionally a bid taker will be assigned to transmit offers coming from that part of the room. Usually you will benefit from having your bid taken by the auctioneer. If the auctioneer and the bid caller accept simultaneous bids at the same figure, the auctioneer will most often take *his* bid at the lower figure and give the bid caller's customer the next advance, if he wants it. If there is no bid caller to cover a blind spot in the room, bidders whose offers are not recognized by the auctioneer have no choice but to move to a different location, or to bid by voice.

The problem with voice bids is that they always seem to convey more urgency than they should. In addition, a vocal bid is a surefire attention grabber that alerts the competition as well as the auctioneer. Knowing against whom one is bidding can be a worthwhile advantage, and it is pretty hard for anyone to remain anonymous while shouting bids loud enough to be heard above the chatter of the audience and the usually amplified voice of the auctioneer. The vocal bidder tends to become an attention center and, aware that many eyes are turned toward him, may feel obliged to behave with a kind of star quality appropriate to the occasion.

It takes a will of iron to drop out of the bidding in a situation like that. The audience, moreover, invariably sides with the vocal bidder, making it practically a betrayal of faith for him to disappoint them by seeming to give up. Their money is on him—the challenger who gamely spoke up from the oblivion of his unfavorable location. He is the underdog who couldn't make it to a good seat among the champions down front, but just the same, he is going to try for the prize. The audience wants him to win! Certainly they will be satisfied with nothing less than a spirited fight to the finish. If he drops out when the going gets rough, they will audibly register disappointment. Under those circumstances, it takes more courage to throw in the towel than it does to toss caution to the winds. It is not unusual for the audience to burst into applause when a lot is taken on a voice bid. Later in the sale, the same buyer might move into a more favorable seat and bid with better effect in unapplauded silence.

Of course, you should call out a bid rather than miss the opportunity to bid for something you want. If you must express a vocal bid, try it at a reduced advance. It might not be accepted, but you will usually be able to revise it, and if nothing else, you will have diminished at least to some degree the surge and impact implicit in a vocal bid.

Most auctioneers have developed a repertoire of techniques that they use to stimulate bidding. The fast knock is one of the most popular, and one of the best. If the audience seems restless and inattentive, and bidding has slowed down, and particularly if the auctioneer is having trouble obtaining his opening demands, he may introduce a lot, ask for a surprisingly low start, and with a sudden call of "Sold!" and a dramatic bang of the hammer, sell on the first bid. Some auctioneers routinely give two or three fast knocks in the course of every sale, just to keep the audience on its toes and the bidding lively.

If you can detect when a fast knock would seem to be in order, and you bid accordingly, you can make some astonishing buys. You can do this only by giving close attention to the auction, listening to the level of conversation in the audience, interpreting the signs of restlessness and inattention —the coughing, the moving about, the yawns, the desultory bidding. You also have to gauge the attitude of the auctioneer. I know one man who, despite the most impeccable control, always smiles a certain quick little smile just as he is about to give a lot a fast knock. I know another whose expression becomes rigidly masklike—the better, I suppose, to contrast with his startling, explosive cry of "Sold!" Don't expect one fast knock to follow another, although there are auctioneers who will give them—just as there are slot machines that are geared to pay two jackpots in succession, if only to prove that the exceptional *can* happen.

If you think that a fast knock is in order, *don't try to cut the first bid.* Negotiation of any sort weakens the effectiveness of the fast knock, and the auctioneer, not about to defeat his purpose, will probably abandon the tactic and routinely sell the lot. Immediately and vigorously bid the full opening demand, and if you have been correct in your observations and deductions, the fast knock will go to your bid. The auctioneer wants to demonstrate the benefit of giving him a quick, enthusiastic, uncut bid. You might as well turn his technique to your occasional advantage.

The shock effect of one fast knock is usually sufficient to stir up lively, competitive bidding on the series of lots that follow. If interest seems to lag again, the auctioneer may try another fast knock, or adopt some different tactic. Deliberate breakage of an item is sometimes resorted to, and can usually be relied on to snap an audience to brisk attention. The sudden, sharp cries of "Yes!" and "Here!" with which bid callers will occasionally punctuate the bidding are like whipcracks to the audience's attention. So are the unexpectedly resounding slams of the auctioneer's hammer. I know one dramatically inclined auctioneer who breaks two or three gavels in the course of each sale. That he maintains a substantial reserve supply of similarly breakable gavels would indicate that his frequent "accidents" are not entirely unplanned.

Even if the sale is being run in a numbered-lot sequence, an auctioneer may suddenly switch to "another consignment," or "a supplementary sheet," in order to vary the offerings if the pace of the sale seems to be slowing down. By introducing a different kind of merchandise, he hopes to involve other members of the audience in the bidding and enliven the sale. He may introduce a number of box lots. "Here's a Klondike for you!" he declares, and suddenly the auction block spills over with assorted items pulled out of a carton or basket. The audience becomes animated. Unusual or unlikely things provoke laughter. And spirited, if not particularly important, bidding. But that does not matter. The change of pace that the auctioneer felt to be needed will have been accomplished. Conversely, he may switch to some of his best lots. "Let's bring out those bronzes—that's what they're waiting for!" Or, "All right, I'm going to put up the Tiffany lamp!" A sudden, concentrated hush falls over the audience. Even those who do not plan to bid on the more costly items are alert, attentive. They know that the bidding may involve several thousand dollars, and they're not about to miss a moment of it. Again, the atmosphere of the sale has been altered.

Some auctioneers will deliberately schedule an important lot early in a sale in order to get the bidding off to a brisk start. Beginning with a major lot is against tradition, but one country auction that we attend always begins at six-thirty sharp, and with one of the most important pieces in the sale. The auctioneer wants to have his best buyers in their seats from the start of the sale—and he succeeds, too. Otherwise the dealers and collectors would come drifting in an hour or two after the auction had begun, and the auctioneer would be without their bids on some of his less significant lots. "If they're here," he said once to explain his custom of opening each sale with an important lot, "they'll buy, but if my big buyers are going to wait until eight-thirty because they think nothing good goes up until then, I might as well give away my first couple of hundred lots."

Even so, the first items up in any sale are seldom the most important. If the catalogue description makes you feel that a particular lot might have been undervalued, the position of the item in the sequence of the sale may often confirm or contradict your hunch.* If it comes up very early, you can usually consider that it is not held in especially high esteem. If you find it scheduled or introduced anywhere from just before the middle up to the final quarter of the sale, you may be surprised at the value that has been set on it. There is a certain curve to the progression of lots at almost every auction—beginning low, rising steadily throughout the first hour or two, cresting sometime before the final third of the sale, and then subsiding gradually. Auctioneers will occasionally continue to present important lots right through to the end of the sale. Most, however, feel it is a mistake to schedule major offerings in the final half-hour, unless they devote the closing portion of the sale to lots of specific character—rugs, perhaps, or silver, or paintings—that would be of interest primarily to a select group of buyers. Seldom will you find the *pièce de résistance* of a sale going up for bids at the end of a long, miscellaneous auction. If you do, bid for it! The auctioneer's miscalculation can sometimes pave the way for a sensational buy. I know one auctioneer who invariably schedules too many lots in his sales, which frequently last, as a result, until one or two o'clock in the morning. Almost everything that goes up during that final hour, when the audience is small and the auctioneer is weary, is apt to be sold for much less than it would have brought at nine or ten in the evening.†

* If you repeatedly attend sales at a gallery, you might find that you can gauge the presumed value of a lot from its position in the exhibition. Of course, some auctioneers will deliberately display a lot under glass or on a pedestal in order to enhance its importance. Just because something is exhibited under lock and key, do not assume that it has value. Conversely, don't neglect those less-well-known lots that might be lying about on open shelves, or in the back room. Frequently that's where the finds are.

† When I asked this auctioneer why he repeatedly assembled sales so extensive that the final lots usually went begging, he explained that the high cost of advertising made it necessary for him to hold fewer but larger sales, at which he realized some lots would fail to achieve their best possible price. He accepts

Often, when a sale includes similar lots of unequal value, the auctioneer will hold the most important lot until the lesser ones have been disposed of. Many potential buyers will be discouraged from bidding on the earlier lots, preferring to concentrate on the final, most significant offering. If you have carefully inspected all the related lots, and are satisfied to own one of the other examples, you might find yourself bidding against shockingly small competition, particularly on the first or second lot in the series.

We recently attended a sale that included a half-dozen lamps with leaded or painted glass shades of varying quality, including two signed HANDEL and one PAIRPOINT. Working his way through the lots in ascending order of value, the auctioneer could not achieve his opening demand on the three less-important lamps, although the Handels and the Pairpoint were quickly bid in at high prices. When they had been disposed of, the auctioneer, by request, reintroduced the first three lamps and managed to sell each of them at several times the figure he had formerly failed to realize. Yet if the man who eventually bought one of those lamps at $100 had given the auctioneer his $25 start the first time that lamp was put up, he might very possibly have owned it on that single bid. Waiting to see if he might be lucky enough to win one of the more important lamps added, perhaps, $75 to the cost of the lamp he eventually bought. On the other hand, suppose he had bid in that first lamp at $25 and later had won one of the more desirable lots. If he could use only one lamp and wished to keep the better of the two, he would have had no trouble realizing a profit on his $25 investment, and if he did not wish to bother disposing of it himself, he could have given it in for auction, where—assuming the under bidder's

the fact that the last fifty to seventy-five lots will sell for less than they should, and that the customers with the patience and fortitude to stay through to the end of the sale will be well rewarded for their persistence.

interest proved the same and the auctioneer's commission was 30 percent—he would have made $38.* Should you find yourself in a similar situation, consider acting accordingly. If the lesser of two items in which you are interested is the first to be sold—and it usually will be—don't pass it by on the chance that you will win the following lot. Remember that most of your competitors will probably be doing the same thing. Which will tend to depress the price at which the first lot will be sold. And that is the time to bid, if one wants to buy wisely. If you should be lucky enough to win the more important lot also, you might try offering the secondary lot to your under bidder, or inquire if the auctioneer will resell it for you.

After John L. Marion sold Van Gogh's *Le Cyprès et l'Arbre en Fleurs* for $1,300,000 in the record-breaking auction of Impressionist and Post-Impressionist paintings at Parke-Bernet on February 25, 1970, he was asked in an interview published in the magazine *Auction* why the two Van Gogh works had been offered early in the sale, and why the more important of the two had been put up first. "When you have two important works by the same artist," the auctioneer replied, "if you begin with the less valuable, people tend to hold back; whereas if the major picture is put up first, all the unsuccessful bidders can try for the second one. . . . After *Le Cyprès et l'Arbre en Fleurs* was sold, the whole atmosphere of the room changed. Bidding became much freer—a lot of people obviously had been waiting to see how the market would be reflected in a painting of the caliber of the Van Gogh."

*Right. The under bid would have been $90. On which the auctioneer's commission at 30 percent would be $27. Add to that the $25 paid for the lamp and the original buyer has a profit of . . . *plus* the lamp that he wanted in the first place. It can and *does* happen.

But not every auctioneer follows that line of reasoning when establishing the sequence in which he will offer lots for sale. Many, in fact, will invariably withhold the more important item, thinking to sustain interest and, thereby, to realize better prices for the preceding lots. Knowing that the result is frequently quite opposite to that can help you make some extraordinary buys.

To bid with maximum effect, adapt your approach to the structure of the sale. Offer fast, low bids on the earliest items, and try giving less than the auctioneer's initial demand—unless you know that he will absolutely refuse a reduced offer. Bid in a similar manner for the first or second in a series of similar lots, if you know that they are being sold in ascending order of importance. Bid the full first demand if you wish to bid early on a major lot that will unquestionably sell at a significantly higher price. (One-third of the expected selling price is a standard opening demand with many auctioneers. Three bids below the hoped-for figure is where others try to open each lot.) If you prefer to withhold your bid until a lot is about to be sold, consider entering with an advance of more than one unit, and do not wait until you are obliged to offer the full amount of your maximum price on your first bid. If the lots in the final third of a sale are of diminishing significance, bid quickly again, and, if possible, in reduced amounts.

Once you have entered the bidding, maintain concentrated contact with the auctioneer or with the bid caller until the bid is closed, or you are ready to retire. Focus in on the auctioneer as if you were trying to take his picture. Don't even look down to check your auction list, or to fumble in your purse, or count your money, or retrieve your pen. The briefest look away could be misinterpreted as a sign of concession on your part. If the auctioneer sells the lot elsewhere, you may or may not be able to argue yourself back into the running through a reopening of the bid. Keep your head up if you are bidding, and keep your eyes on the auctioneer. You looked at the lots during the exhibition, so after a fast glance to establish the lot on the block is the one on which you want to bid, you have no need to sit staring at it. The auctioneer should have your full attention throughout the sale of any lot on which you are bidding—not only while you bid, but also while he takes bids against you. If he comes back to you for a bid and finds that you are looking away, or down, or not responding immediately, he could instantly close the lot on your rival's bid. And once he declares the lot sold, he might not be inclined to sell it again. Some auctioneers will. Some absolutely will not. Auction tradition decrees that "Sold" means *sold*. Even the most volubly disappointed bidder is liable to be unsuccessful at flouting it. Occasionally an auctioneer might want very much to reopen a bid, but will not risk slowing the pace of the sale, or taxing the patience of his audience. The best way to avoid disappointment is to do nothing that might be interpreted as a sign of concession. It isn't necessary to carry on like a manic enthusiast. Just watch and listen.

Sooner or later you will attend one of those auctions at which a minimum number of bids will be required before any lot—or possibly before some of the more important lots—will be sold. Certain auctioneers will refuse to sell anything on a single bid. Others will sell less valuable lots on one bid, and insist on achieving a second or even a third bid throughout the balance of the sale. Many auctioneers protect themselves and their consignors by demanding a minimum of two bids, and will refuse to permit the initial bidder to make the second offer. Without a legitimate competitive bid, they insist that the lot fails and must be removed from the sale.

Other auctioneers operating under the two-bid system will acknowledge the second bid of the original bidder and, if no other offer follows, sell on that basis.

Occasionally the second advance will be accepted from another member of the group from which the first offer was taken, although many auctioneers will refuse to do that, insisting that it does not constitute a truly competitive bid. Do not, therefore, think that you can cleverly counter this tactic by having your companion bid against you. You can, however (and usually with expectation of success), ask someone sitting immediately in front of you to enter the second bid against you. This tactic presumes (1) that you are not sitting in the first row; (2) that the person whose aid you enlist is absolutely uninterested in bidding for the lot in question; (3) that you have not previously resorted to this stratagem in the course of the sale; (4) that you know you can trust your accomplice to accept the lot for you and to surrender it to you: once it is knocked down to him, it becomes his legal property, you know, and he might decide to keep it, or to resell it to you at a substantial profit.

You want to ask someone sitting ahead of you not only because it saves you the noticeable and awkward business of turning around, but also because you then can see that the cooperative bid is actually given and acknowledged. You could ask the person seated beside you, but that is such an obvious ploy that it almost invites defeat.

Perhaps the simple thing would seem to be to ask your assistant bidder to make the original bid for you, giving you the winning second bid and keeping the record of ownership clear. This would be ideal if you knew that you and your colleague would enter the only bids. Suppose, however, that someone else enters the second bid ahead of you? You can then enter the bidding only with the third offer, which might or might not take the lot. Eliminate your colleague's initial bid. Assume that your competitor's interest stands. You wait, giving the other bidder the opportunity to make the initial bid. The required second bid then is yours. And if your opponent elects not to continue, you win the lot.

What you want to ensure is that there will be an initial bid, and that in the event it is not given by a competitor, you are free to make it at the point of your choice. And that if there is no increase on your opening, a quasicompetitor will enter a second bid on your behalf. Asking your colleague to offer the first bid might only increase the competition. Additionally, you probably could not control the point at which he would bid, although his increase on your bid would be a standard increment. If you should succeed in this bit of two-bid hokum, be sufficiently clever not to congratulate each other, or to make your appreciation apparent. Later in the sale, your assistant could ask the bookkeeper to transfer that particular lot to your account. The bookkeeper might ask to have your confirmation that you plan to honor the charge. If anything is said, you can always explain that you purchased the lot from your friend, who has changed his mind, or perhaps spent more than he realized. It might be best not to ask your accomplice to pay for the lot, or to give him the money to pay for it—unless, of course, he happens to be someone you know well enough to trust and impose upon.

The same technique can be used to win lots auctioned off under a three-bid requirement. It is still the second bid of which you want to be sure. You make the first bid. A competitor—or failing that, your colleague, by prearrangement —makes the second. The third bid, then, is yours. There's no guarantee that it will be the final bid, but you have secured for yourself the first bid that possibly could be. Lots of people will make the second offer on a three-bid lot—simply, I suppose, because it gives them a chance to bid on something that they know they cannot possibly buy. But just in case, it is good to have a confederate up your sleeve—or better yet, seated in front of you.

On any lot requiring a minimum of two or three bids, it is important to be prepared to make the first offer, even though you know that it cannot take the lot. If no one else opens: bid! One bid can generally be expected to induce another. If it doesn't, you, hopefully, have made some private arrangement to guarantee that it will. But if the auctioneer fails to secure a starting bid, all your careful strategy will have been wasted on a passed lot.

Don't give the second bid on a three-bid lot unless it is obvious that without it, the lot will fail. If the second offer is two bidding units below your established maximum bid, you can make it, knowing that you can come back to bid in the full amount if a competitor enters a bid against you. Again, you may or may not wish to enlist the aid of a confederate to offer bid number three in the event no genuine competition develops. If the price still seems reasonably low, and you don't mind spending a few dollars to keep the record straight, you might want to bid again in order to secure the lot. The drawback then is that by keeping the bidding open a bit longer, you risk encouraging others to come in against you.

I think that the three-bid requirement, which, happily, is encountered with less and less frequency, is sufficiently unfair to justify a little friendly collaboration among bidders. A two-bid minimum is standard at many auctions, and although it is a bit frustrating—especially if it is indiscriminately applied to many minor lots, which, consequently, remain unsold—can be justified as an attempt to ensure competitive bidding. Some consignors, in fact, will insist that the auctioneer require at least a second bid before a lot can be sold.

(Some auctioneers, of course, unwilling to be told how to conduct a sale, will suggest that the consignment be placed elsewhere.)

The requirement of a second or third bid becomes somewhat absurd if the auctioneer is employing shills. The under bids then come freely, but frequently result in numerous unsold lots.*

The advance, or order, bid, also known as a sealed bid, is another legitimate auction technique that, although often legitimately employed, can also be used as a bit of covert running of genuine bidders. (*See Chapter 6: How to Avoid Bidding Against Yourself.*) This is not the same as a reserve bid, which represents a restriction on the part of the consignor, establishing a minimum below which a lot may not be sold.

The consignor's reserve is not necessarily the auctioneer's opening demand. An auctioneer may elect to start a lot substantially under the owner's reserve. Should the bidding not reach the reserve price, the auctioneer will be obliged to withdraw the lot, provided fewer than the required number of bids have been taken, or to bid it in for the house. Even the most legitimate auctioneer must ocasionally do this, entering a phantom bid on the consignor's behalf. If he receives an increase from the audience, the auctioneer may have to continue to bid for the owner until the reserve has been achieved. The responsible auctioneer, of course, will insist that any

* Not surprisingly, a lot that has been knocked down to a shill can sometimes be found among the offerings at a later auction. If your patience outlasts the auctioneer's, you might eventually be able to bid it in at a surprisingly low figure, even as you might pick up an end-of-the-season bargain in a retail shop. The risk is about the same—someone might buy it before you get to it; you are, basically, choosing from the rejects. But that is not always a bad thing to do. When an auctioneer has offered a particular lot more than once, he will often waive the three-bid requirement and, like a retailer taking a markdown on slow-moving inventory, open the bidding with a lower start each time. Unless the piece is withdrawn by its consignor, the auctioneer will eventually close it out for a fast, fair bid, if only to avoid having to repeat it at another later sale.

reserve to which he agrees be set at a reasonable level, and refuse to handle consignments carrying unrealistic reserves.

An order bid is something quite different, and a bidding technique of which you might occasionally want to take advantage. What it represents is an offer on your part to have bids entered for you up to and including a certain amount (your established maximum bid) on a particular lot. The auctioneer, or one of his assistants, will bid for you, and enter bids in competition with those taken from the audience. I do not know any gallery that charges the buyer for this service. Properly handled, the order bid is not introduced at its full value as an opening offer. An auctioneer who does that actually is exploiting the advance bidder by trying to use his best offer as a springboard to higher bidding. Moreover, he squanders the full amount of the order, should the lot go to the advance bidder on that single bid. Auctioneers have defended this tactic by saying that they are merely trying to save time, to keep the sale moving. Some suggest that by immediately bidding the full value of the order, they knock out trivial competition that otherwise might needlessly have prolonged the auction. "It's boring for people to sit while things go through a whole cycle of bidding and then are knocked down on a sealed bid. Half the time they figure you're just faking. It's better to throw the whole shebang at them right off the bat. Then, if they don't want to top it, you knock it down, one-two-three, to the order." The explanation that the advance bidder would have been willing to bid up to his maximum had he been present at the sale does not seem satisfactory, however, since competitive open bidding might never have reached that amount.

In handling an order bid for the customer's best advantage, the auctioneer will enter competitive bids at increments no greater than those taken from the audience. He may advise those present that an order bid has been taken on the lot about to be sold, and indicate who will bid for the absent party. Regardless of the amount of the advance bid, the auctioneer will ask for the same opening bid he would ordinarily set for the lot. If he fails to receive an offer, he then might take that amount from his advance bid. The bidding then continues until any audience interest that has been aroused is exhausted, at which point the lot is sold to the order account for the amount of the next regular bid. If the sealed bid is exhausted while active bidding continues from the audience, the auctioneer may or may not elect to announce that the prior bid has been passed.

You might want to leave an advance bid for a lot in a sale that you cannot attend, or if there are only one or two items in which you are interested in what would seem to be an otherwise unrewarding auction. If you have traveled several hours to attend the exhibition and find only a few lots on which you would like to bid, you might not want to repeat the journey to attend the sale. In that case, ask the auctioneer to enter an order bid for you—but keep in mind that if you win the lot, you will probably have to repeat the trip to collect it.

There might also be occasions on which you would like to bid anonymously. In such instances, you can ask the auctioneer to handle a sealed bid for you, even though you are present in the audience. Why would you want your identity unknown? That sort of thing, you might think, is all well and good if you are J. Paul Getty, or Aristotle Onassis, or Elizabeth Taylor, or the Director of the Cleveland Museum. But you and I—probably not famous, not legendary, not recognized, not spectacular in terms of wealth or beauty or expertise—why would we want not to be recognized? Perhaps to protect us from our auction friends and enemies. Many auction bids are entered for emotional rather than rational reasons. "He thinks he has to have everything . . . well, I'm not going to let him get away with it!" is heard more often than you might expect in a company of adults. Or "If she's bidding on it, it must be something good, because she knows what she's doing!" Or "If he thinks he's going to take that away from me as he did that dresser at the last auction, he's going to be surprised!" You can also save embarassment if you know that you and a friend are going to be in competition for a particular lot.*

Some unethical auctioneers will use the order bid as a device to increase prices. Either they will open a lot with the full value of a genuine bid, or they will announce advance bids that they actually do not hold. Some believe that the declaration of an advance bid serves to enhance the desirability of a lot. Others use it simply as a protection against achieving less than a specified reserve, or for a shield behind which they run up legitimate bidding.

Order bids also can represent blanket advance bids whereby a dealer will authorize an auctioneer to bid in unspecified lots up to a certain total value. Again, an auctioneer may use an "order account" as a repository for any unsold lots that have failed to achieve a desired minimum, or on which he had successfully been bidding up someone in the audience. Some order accounts are genuine and represent years of mutually profitable association between an auctioneer and a dealer. Others are frauds and, if they represent purchases of any sort, may indicate only buying-in by the auctioneer. The mythical order account is nothing but a shill that isn't there. Smart auctioneers seldom have to resort to it. Those who do

* There are no friends at auction," remember, but in the event that you would like to have a few to cherish during those hours you spend outside the gallery, the anonymity of an advance bid can lessen the strain that sometimes taxes even the strongest of bonds. If your friend wins the lot, you then avoid the accusation of having bid him up. If you win it, you can explain that when you realized that it was in competition with him, it was too late for you to rescind your advance bid. Don't be surprised if he later tries the same line on you. Don't be angry, either.

usually give themselves away sooner or later. If you feel that you are bidding in any sort of running situation, it is important to stay within your previously established maximum bids. Deliberately losing an occasional lot will help you discourage the auctioneer from trying to run you on others.

Conversely, if a sale includes one lot that you are anxious to buy, and you have not previously bought from the auctioneer, it is a good idea to bid in one or two earlier lots in order to introduce yourself to him. Even better strategy would be to win a few lots and retire unsuccessfully from others. It isn't necessary to take everything in the sale. You will be amazed how quickly the auctioneer will recognize you after even an insignificant purchase. He'll remember you at the next auction, too.

Inevitably, there will be a bid that you instantly regret. Call, "Withdrawn," and tell yourself that you will be more cautious next time around. Very few bidders realize that any offer can be withdrawn as long as the auctioneer has not acknowledged it as the winning bid and closed the lot with the word "Sold," or his particular variant thereof. No bid previous to that represents a firm commitment on the part of the bidder. Consequently, although retracting a bid will not win you a place on the auctioneer's list of All-Time Favorites, it is a right that you enjoy until the lot has been knocked down to you and the contract closed by the auctioneer's acceptance of your offer, signified almost universally by a call of "Sold."

If you do wish to withdraw a bid, do so at once, even if it seems obvious that a competitor is about to take the bid away from you. For one thing, it would be unfair for his bid to be inflated by the amount of yours. Additionally, if he should decide to rescind his bid, you might be left with the final offer on the item, and should the auctioneer then quickly knock it down to you, it might be awkward to withdraw at that point. You could probably accomplish this, but why bother, when it is so easy to call, "Withdrawn"? Actually, your under bid would have to be confirmed before the lot could be knocked down to you, and most auctioneers will take pains to establish that your offer stands. "Do you want it at————?" you will usually be asked. Even though you know you have the right then to refuse the lot, you might find it embarrassing to do so, since that would constitute an admission of indiscreet bidding. So, of course, does the withdrawal of a bid while the lot is still up for sale—but it is much more difficult to say "no" to a lot that is being offered to you alone, particularly since you were sufficiently interested to have initiated at least one impulsive bid. As with most mistakes, the more quickly an undesired bid is corrected, the better.

There remains one important aspect of bidding that, unless clearly understood, can lead to misunderstanding, disappointment, unpleasantness, embarrassment, and sometimes forfeiture of a purchase. Frequently a lot includes more than one item. It might be a pair of candlesticks. Or a set of six chairs. Or a dozen dinner plates. It could consist of two or more totally unrelated paintings. Or three souvenir spoons. It could be a set of draperies. A bundle of linen napkins. Seven glasses. Five knives. Two swords. Four—well, it could be anything that the auctioneer or his cataloguer happens to lump together. Of what the lots consist is something you should have determined at the exhibition. What you need to be very sure of at the sale is *how* these multiple lots are being sold. Is your bid a single offer for everything in the lot? Or is it for one unit of the lot? And if it is, are you required to accept the remaining units at the same price? Or do you have the privilege of taking one, all, or as many as you choose?

Considering how important it is to know under which of these various conditions you are bidding, and how easy it is to find out, it is astonishing that at least once at nearly any auction, someone bids happily along until he discovers that his winning bid, for which he thought he would receive the entire lot, represented the price he agreed to pay for only one item, and that he is expected to make good for that amount multiplied by the number of items in the lot.

Most often the auctioneer will announce that a lot consisting of two or more items is to be sold by the lot, by the pair, or by the piece. If he says "So much a piece and take the pair," then your purchase price for the lot is double your bid, and you must accept both items. Or he may say, "So much each and two [or four, or six, or whatever] times the money!" Same meaning. If the auctioneer announces, "I'm selling these per each, with the privilege," then your winning bid is the unit price that you agree to pay for one or as many of the items from the lot as you elect to purchase. There are countless variations of these phrases; the important thing is to listen closely and understand exactly what is meant.

If you don't understand the terms under which you are bidding: *ask*. Don't hold up your hand to ask—you might be thought to be making a bid. Ask aloud, loud enough to be heard, precisely how the lot is being sold. Chances are that the auctioneer would rather stop and explain than have you bid without fully realizing your responsibility. For one thing, if you think you are bidding a single price for a multiple lot, you will obviously be willing to bid much higher than a competitor who correctly understands that the bidding is on a unit basis. He might be willing to pay up to $500 on a lot consisting of four items. Accordingly, since bids are being taken on a unit basis, he would drop out at $125. You, on the other hand, thinking yourself to be bidding one sum for the entire lot, might gladly advance to $200 or more. Until the auctioneer called, "Sold!" and you learned that you had obligated yourself to pay four times your winning bid. Usually, red with embarrassment, you will say, "Eight hundred dollars?" or whatever, and the auctioneer will explain what he would gladly have explained earlier if you had taken the time to ask him. Most often he will release you from your bid. So, other than looking a little foolish, you will not have suffered any great harm. Except that you might not want to forfeit the lot. After all, you were interested enough to bid it in, however mistakenly. And maybe you had even planned to bid up to $600. Instead of the bargain you thought you had at $200, you now are faced with the choice between paying $200 over your established maximum and losing out entirely. It would take a lot of nerve to bid again on the lot if it were put up for sale a second time. Some auctioneers, in fact, might refuse to accept your bids after having given you relief because of a misunderstanding. On the other hand, had you correctly understood the bidding basis, you could have topped your competitor's total $500 maximum and perhaps taken the lot at or below your best offer.

Because two items naturally belong together, don't just assume that they are being sold together for a single price. A creamer and a sugar bowl on a tray can be one item or three, depending on how the auctioneer wants to sell the lot. I have even bid on each of a pair of candlesticks. This kind of bidding has the advantage of making the lot seem to be selling for less than it is, which the auctioneer, no doubt, feels will encourage continued bidding. And it is true that if items are being auctioned in this manner, you have to do a lot of fast multiplication to distinguish your actual offer from the amount of the bid called. I suppose it is frequently misleading to sit before an auction block on which twenty-four dinner plates are displayed and to hear bids entered at $10, $15, $20. How wonderfully tempting! Ask yourself if it would be equally tempting if the bids given were $240, $360, $480. Or $600.

Because if you still feel tempted, *that*—not $25—would be the true value of your next bid.

It is difficult to calculate a fair "by the piece" bid on a lot consisting of two parts of which one is in some way inferior. Auctioneers will frequently lot together one perfect and one imperfect item and then take unit bids, rightly expecting that the appeal of the more desirable part will enhance the price offered for the other. Obviously, you have to consider the extent of the damage to the imperfect item, and its potential value—or lack of value—to arrive at any kind of reasonable estimate. If you decide that $50 would be a fair price for the good item, don't mistakenly bid that amount *for each*. (It is extremely easy to do this, since you would probably have that amount in mind.) If you calculate that $50 would be the right bid for the perfect item and $25 for the damaged one, remember that $75 would be your total offer for the lot—which makes your per-each maximum bid come to $37.50, since you will be paying equally for two items of unequal value. This is the only reasonable way to determine a bidding figure—to calculate the combined worth of the lot and divide it by the number of items included in it. The result is the figure that you bid. It would be correct to seem to undervalue the better item in such a lot. The alternative would be to overpay for the less desirable one.

Each time a lot is knocked down to you, record the price; a description of the item, including of how many pieces it consists; and the lot number, if there is one. Do this immediately. Do not try to rely on your always-infallible memory. If the item is delivered to you immediately, and you pay cash for it, the receipt you obtain at that time will do. Otherwise, since you are going to have to claim your purchases at the end of the sale—or, perhaps, even a day or two after the sale—you will want to be sure that your records are accurate as to item, condition and price. If you have prepared a list of lots on which you had planned to bid, you will need only to circle the numbers of the lots that you win, and note the amount of your final bid. (Be sure to record the actual price in a way that distinguishes it from your bidding estimates. And since you will sometimes want to record the prices of lots that you did not win, be careful that those figures do not get confused with your winning bids.) If you are working from an annotated catalogue, you might find it becoming a little crowded with these additions. Next time, you will probably take the trouble to prepare a separate list for yourself. Some buyers jot down their purchases on their numbered cards. Nothing very wrong with that—provided you have been given a numbered card. Go to one auction at which bidding numbers are issued on paddles and you will attend the next with a notebook, just as we now do.

There really aren't any friends at auction. You will find that you make new friends, and that many others whom you meet are friendly, but when a friend tells you that he failed to win a particular lot because he "didn't want to bid against you," it might be a good idea to remind him that you would not consider that an act of personal betrayal. Otherwise, you are going to feel pretty self-conscious the next time you find yourself bidding against *him*. Anytime someone says, "I knew you were bidding for it, and I didn't want to bid against you," he is implicitly obligating you not to bid in competition with him. If you start worrying about such matters of hurt feelings and damaged friendships, you are going to start losing lots you might otherwise have purchased. When someone attempts to use that tactic on me, I always say, "Don't feel that way. If you are interested in a lot, bid for it. I would. It isn't anything personal, you know. Besides, my not bidding couldn't guarantee that you would win. And it would be a shame for both of us to miss out."

Of course, there are groups of friends or associates or even competitors who form rings by agreeing among themselves not to bid against one another. Most often a ring will be made up of dealers who specialize in similar merchandise: rugs, or silver, or jewels, or furs, or Orientalia; although it could be anything—typewriters, toiletries, furniture, you-name-it. Usually the members of an auction ring share a certain expertise, which they feel gives them advantages not enjoyed by the average buyer. By designating one member of their group to bid in all lots in which there is interest, the ring reduces competitive bidding by coordinating what otherwise would be conflicting offers. Thus, by prior agreement, Dealer A, Dealer B and Dealer C will refrain from bidding, while Dealer D, bidding on behalf of the ring, enters a single bid that is three increments lower than it would have been if each dealer had acted independently. After the auction, the members of the ring will usually hold a closed auction of their own at which the various lots are resold. The difference between the price paid at public auction and the final price bid in by a member of the ring will be divided evenly among the membership. Thus, if Dealer A were to obtain a lot for $100 over the bid at which the ring obtained it, and the ring consisted of four members, Dealer A's share of the $100 difference would reduce his actual cost by $25. The operation of a ring thus not only serves to depress prices in the auction room, but also offers members an opportunity to do a little profit sharing as well. A clever manipulator can, in fact, emerge from a ring re-auction without making a single purchase, yet taking a substantial profit from his noninvestment. It is his "reward," so to speak, for not bidding against his colleagues.

In order to operate effectively, a ring must include a generous percentage of all potential buyers for any lot in which there is interest. As a rule, auctioneers hate dealer rings almost as much as they hate refunds, or the mention of shills. I know one auctioneer who refuses to accept bids from members of a ring if he finds their tactics jeopardizing the success of a sale. "There are ten of you in a silver ring there, and if you won't give me a decent advance on these lots, I'm not going to take your bids!" another auctioneer once declared. "I can get very blind where members of a ring are concerned," a third said. "If they want to play games, so can I."

Buyers will sometimes say that a private customer doesn't have a chance if he is competing with an auction ring. This is precisely the attitude that members of a ring strive to encourage. And it is not valid. The successful ring is organized to depress prices. By eliminating several potentially competitive bidders, the ring actually *helps* an informed buyer who knows the value of the lot and what he might reasonably expect to pay for it. It is much more difficult to win a lot from a capricious amateur who feels he must own something regardless of how high he has to bid than from a tightly organized ring of professionals who will not exceed a realistic price. Additionally, most auctioneers will give preference *away* from a ring.

A private buyer can almost always afford to top the bid of a dealer—although he may not sufficiently appreciate his more favorable position. A dealer must allow at least a minimal markup to cover his expenses, which include the not-inconsiderable cost of time spent acquiring merchandise. Add to that such ordinary items of overhead as transportation, salaries and rent, and you can quickly see that the dealer is in a less favorable bidding position than a knowledgeable private buyer.

The strength from which the dealer bids, of course, is his experience and (presumed) expertise. The private buyer who bothers to inform himself about values can usually safely outbid his professional competitors. And that awesome auction ring is usually nothing but a group of dealers acting as one. Seen as what it is—a group of buyers with precisely the same objective that you have: to bid in a lot at the lowest price at which it can be obtained—the ring loses much of its legendary power. You might want to remember this the next time someone tells you, "We won't be able to get anything tonight. There's nothing but dealers here . . ." or, "Forget about the rugs, because those five men in the back row are all in a ring against us!" If you know what you want to buy, and have a fair appreciation of its worth, you should actually be glad to hear that when you set out to buy at auction.

5 HOW TO MAKE A KILLING

MOST OF the mistakes that I have made at auction occurred because I thought I was about to make a killing. It is easy to be lured into that exciting state of optimistic expectancy. Practically everyone dreams of getting something if not for nothing, then at most for only a fraction of its true worth. And newspaper and magazine reports of fabulous auction buys lend credibility to that tantalizing possibility. Quite early in your auction-going career, you will probably find yourself approaching each sale pretty much as Lord Carnarvon must have felt as he unsealed the tomb of Tut-ankh-amen. Friends will tell you of the fantastic purchases they have made—how they found pure gold amid the rubbish. Auctioneers will dazzle you with stories about the $1 bundle of old books that was found to include a valuable first edition. Rare coins turn up in penny banks like *Mayflower* ancestors at a DAR tea. A packet of old postcards yields a $1,000 stamp. You will hear about trunks of old papers in which Lincoln letters were discovered. And box lots of worthless glass that included one perfect signed Tiffany vase.* As for paintings and sculpture—

* This happened. Not, alas, to me, but to a friend. He paid $5 for a box lot. He later sold the vase to a dealer for $500. Hardly a killing, but certainly a not-bad return on his auction investment. Job lots, about which more later, are

the legendary killings provide auction lore with some of its most dramatic highlights.

The trouble is that these reports of fabulous auction buys encourage one to feel that any lot put up for bids stands a good chance of having been part of the lost treasure of the Incas. Any portrait in dark browns and oily yellow is thought to be a neglected masterpiece. Late Japanese porcelain acquires the potential value of priceless Sung ware. The desire to make a killing adds luster to reproductions, conceals flaws and can transmute lead into bronze more effectively than that magical stone the alchemists sought.

Truthfully, there are few killings to be made. Treasures there are, and available at auction—often available *only* at auction—but seldom without proper evaluation. Everyone is alert to art. Discovered masterpieces and attic treasures make news precisely because they are so rare. Important works of art are not languishing in every dusty barn. If Grandma hid something in the attic, chances are excellent that she knew precisely what she was storing away. And even if she didn't, the man who comes to auction off her property probably will. And if he doesn't, it is to be expected that at least one of your competitors will.

I stood in the rain for three hours one afternoon while the contents of an old house were being auctioned. At the inspection, I had seen a fine American Queen Anne lowboy hidden away under the eaves in the attic. A treasure! I anticipated hours of patient refinishing, years and years of prideful ownership. And at such an otherwise uninspiring sale, I thought I would pick it up for next to nothing. It seemed obvious that the auctioneer had neglected the piece—all the presumably "better" furniture had been displayed downstairs. The lowboy would easily have brought over $1,000 if it had been

---

always worth inspecting, even if they are not always worth buying. Never be afraid to look.

refinished. As it stood, it might have realized better than $500 in a sale where it was properly regarded. I felt confident that I might be able to take it for $50, since the rain had reduced the crowd to a shivering handful, the auctioneer seemed impatient to get through the sale, and none of the drenched competition looked especially wealthy or wise. Prices, as the sale progressed, were encouragingly low. I bid in two lots I really didn't want because they were going for a few dollars and I wanted to introduce myself to the auctioneer before I began to bid for the lowboy.

Hours later, after a parade of broken Grand Rapids furniture, chipped china and damaged glass, the lowboy was carelessly carried out onto the porch. By that time, I thought I might own it for as little as $10, although, recognizing a find when I found one, I was—sportingly—prepared to go somewhat higher.

I quickly discovered that I need not have worried. "Well, I guess I don't have to say anything about this," the auctioneer said, slamming the palm of his hand loudly against the top of the piece.

He was right. He didn't. One of the least impressive members of the audience (it is hard to look distinguished under a dripping umbrella) opened the bid at $100 and we were off and running. At $650 the lowboy finally went to the original bidder, and I went to get dry clothes and a cup of hot coffee.

The point of this bit of personal reminiscence is not that it is futile to attend auctions on rainy afternoons. (Actually, that is one of the most favorable times for good buys.) Or that no matter how clever you happen to be, someone is apt to be equally clever. (Include the auctioneer in that. Remember, he doesn't make his money by neglecting valuable pieces.) What it all boils down to is that if you go to an auction with the expectation of making a killing, you are probably courting disappointment. You have reference books and price guides. So have your competitors. Some of your rivals, moreover, may have years of experience to draw upon. And of collectors, beware! Where their specialty is concerned, their expertise is usually unsurpassable. And price becomes secondary to possession if a lot includes something that will enrich their collection. In fact, the high price of a recent acquisition can actually increase the worth of an entire collection, since auction records are often taken as standards of value for appraisals.*

But if it is difficult to make a killing, it is at least possible to make a find. Auction rooms are packed with finds, and once you have accepted the fact that compared with unrecognized Renoirs, hen's teeth are plentiful, you can have a very good and profitable time exploring and bidding and buying.

The problem is one of attitude. It is hard *not* to expect to make a killing. People who enjoy buying at auction tend to be enthusiastic, optimistic and willing to take chances. While we might never risk our hard-earned pennies at the tables in Las Vegas, we will gamble on a Houdon sculpture, or a Hepplewhite sideboard. Gamble first that we will win the bid, and second, that we will have bought wisely. Our careful inspection will have removed much of the risk, but none of the excitement implicit in the second instance. And, let's face it, the elements of chance and challenge contribute much to the pleasure of buying at auction. If he is absolutely frank with you, even the most jaded auction buff will admit that

---

* Many stories are told about the famous dealer Duveen, who once, finding himself in possession of more than he wanted of the works of a particular artist, purchased yet another at auction, bidding it in at a record-breaking price. Somewhat later, having disposed of the earlier examples for more than even he would formerly have dared to ask, Duveen revealed that his auction buy had been made solely to stimulate the market for an artist in whose work interest had been declining. A famous collector of paperweights recently revealed that price is a matter of little consequence to him, since record purchases only enhance the value of his entire collection.

somewhere in the back of his mind glimmers a spark of hope that with a ridiculously low bid, he will be clever enough to win something of value.

But if you attend every auction with the mental set that treasure is about to be yours for a minimal bid, you will probably find that you are inclined to bid more than you should for lots that are worth less than you thought; and less than you need to in order to win important items. Expecting to make a killing, you might find that you have only made a number of unwise purchases.

Once I bought a Rembrandt etching for $35. Beautiful! One of the first four states of *Ecce Homo*. Unsigned, of course, since the name appears over the right arch only in the seventh state. The blacks were properly velvety. The lines, correctly burred. The plate marks were just visible within the rather poorly cut mat. This was no picture torn out of a book! I couldn't believe my luck. And, of course, I shouldn't have. If I hadn't *expected* to make a killing, I might have approached the picture with a far more critical eye.

"There are quite a few of these reproductions around," I was told when I took my treasure to be appraised. "One might bring about twenty-five dollars. I'm sorry that it isn't worth ten thousand dollars." Not only had I not made a killing: I had actually overpaid for something I would never have purchased off a gallery wall.

But consider the situation in which I found the picture: a magnificent old mansion in a community of quiet wealth, where the estate of a teacher of art was being sold at auction. For $2 at that sale, I could have bought a stack of original watercolors that spread three inches thick over the top of the grand piano! The entire contents of the basement went for $20, and included bronze wall sconces, chandeliers, andirons, and stacks of books and magazines that might have paid great dividends of pleasure. But I was blind to everything but that "Rembrandt." I can't think how many interesting lots I let pass while I concentrated on that etching.

I tried to restore my deflated ego by reminding myself that someone else had bid $30 on the same picture. But that did not help a great deal, because hand in hand with that rationalization came the realization that my opponent, at least, had been wise enough to retire after $30, while I, if the bid had not closed at $35, would probably have gone to some ridiculous limit, thinking all the time that I was making a killing.

I still look at the picture from time to time, and tell myself that it was a good lesson to learn early in my auction-going career. Who can say how much that $35 mistake has saved me?

Because it is possible at auction to buy something for less than it is worth, it does not necessarily follow that anything bought at auction will be worth more than one pays. The chance to make a killing is so seductive a lure that it tempts one to overpayment. Ulysses had his shipmates' ears filled with wax while, lashed to the mast, he permitted himself to listen to the song of the Sirens. If the thought of making a killing at auction stirs in you an urge to raise your hand and bid and bid and bid: restrain yourself with a reminder that good things usually *look* good, that they seldom go cheap, and that when they do, there is usually something wrong with them.

If the Sirens' song still echoes through those cold caverns of reason, try arming yourself against disappointment by remembering some of the unwise auction buys that have been made. The legendary killings get publicized, but one seldom hears about the fakes, the reproductions and the cheap imports that frequently get sold at auction. None of us likes to talk about his mistakes. Remember my "Rembrandt," take a second look, and think before you bid.

Ask yourself if the "treasure" makes sense in context with the balance of the sale. If no other lot seems to belong with it, be suspicious. Be equally suspicious if too many other lots resemble it. Just because one lot is an obvious reproduction, don't reject the possibility that your treasure is real. On the other hand, if many of the lots seem less than genuine, don't expect any of them to be valuable. There *is* auction merchandise—furniture, decorations, carpets, etc.—made specifically for sale at auction. Vivid colors and shiny finishes frequently mask inferior workmanship, while the excitement of the sale situation, stimulated by the auctioneer's skillful techniques and the expectation that any auction buy will be a bargain, frequently produces prices that are in excess of prevailing retail values.

And there are *new* imports!*

We recently traveled for several hours to attend an auction that had been advertised enticingly. An estate was to be sold —someone's name was listed in the announcement—that included household furnishings and an elaborate collection consisting of a "tremendous quantity" of carvings in ivory, jade, lapis, rose quartz, carnelian and other semiprecious stones. There would also be antique porcelains, bronzes and other interesting lots. The "tremendous quantity" of hardstone carvings made us feel that the lots might have been assembled in an importer's warehouse rather than from a connoisseur's estate, but the sale was being conducted by an auctioneer we had never met, and sounded interesting enough to justify the trip.

The instant we walked into the auction room, we knew that

---

* There are *old* imports too, but that is something else again. The imports to be alert to are those contemporary manufactures that turn up at auction where they sometimes masquerade as "antiques." European and Far Eastern factories are supplying pseudo-antiques to gift shops and auction rooms throughout the United States. There's nothing wrong with these imports, of course, provided you don't buy them for "old," and at antiques prices.

our first suspicion had been correct: some of the furniture might have been removed from a private home, but the entire "tremendous quantity" of hardstone carvings consisted of recent imports of no special distinction, and the porcelains were principally Hong Kong hand-painted rather than old rose medallion. It was an appalling display. To make the insult worse, the town had provided a uniformed policeman to guard the gallery and enhance, no doubt, the purported value of the dubious collection.

We decided to stay for at least the early part of the sale, just to see if anyone was actually going to bid seriously for the genuine, but neither old nor very good, lots. Similar (in fact, *identical*) items could be bought at any of a dozen souvenir and import shops in New York. The "ivories" were not hand-carved, but molded ivory "composition"—which is politely saying, "ivory dust." The stoppers of the "antique" snuff bottles were encircled by clean, new cork. The tiny wands, or dippers, had obviously never been used. The brass linings of jars and boxes gleamed in shiny newness. Bits of excelsior, straw and other packing materials underscored the "fresh off the boat" message.* There was no question that the majority of the lots going up for sale that night were items the auctioneer had brought in to sell at, or above, an established price. None of the merchandise would go below cost. Nothing would be stolen, except the buyer's confidence when he discovered the true quality of the lots he had purchased.

The auctioneer was defensive from the moment we asked

---

* Yes, estates also get packed for storage or transportation, but usually in newspaper, or tissue paper, or shredded paper, or—more recently—amid pebbles of Styrofoam. Excelsior and straw are the stuff of overseas shipments. Telltale traces of them in the interiors of new-looking things should cause the kind of suspicion with which brunette wives in 1930s films would discover a blond hair clinging to their husband's lapel: it might not prove anything, but it certainly suggests that someone could be cheating.

to be shown some of the items which, to further the illusion of great value, were displayed in locked cases. We had arrived an hour before sale time, since the advertisement had indicated that the exhibition would be at that time. "I don't like to have people handle these things the night of the sale," he said as he reluctantly handed us the first piece that we had requested. I was surprised, since that had been the time announced for inspection. When I mentioned this, the auctioneer said that the advertisement had simply said, ON VIEW, which was not quite the same thing. "Do you mean," I asked, "that you would rather we bid for these items without first having carefully examined them?" The gallery was posted with signs declaring that all sales were final, and that cash only would be accepted. How wise, in those circumstances, I thought, and how difficult, then, to obtain satisfaction if one later wanted to return something that proved to have been incorrectly represented. The auctioneer wouldn't want to risk having someone stop payment on a check if he refused to go along with an adjustment.

Yet when the sale began, people who otherwise displayed fundamental good sense bid with competitive enthusiasm and paid good cash for their specious treasures, and received their purchases as gratefully as a well-mannered hungry child might accept a cake.

We watched for an hour, until it became unbearable as lot after lot either was knocked down on a fake bid or sold for many times its actual value. If the buyers had not thought it possible to steal a fine hand-carved ivory for a fraction of its worth, they might have been more skeptical. In their eagerness to make a killing, they allowed themselves to be robbed.

A self-confessed confidence woman with whom I once worked on a book told me how she and her partner had pulled the "pigeon drop" on countless lonely elderly women. One of them would spot the pigeon in a department store or a restaurant and begin a conversation with her, setting her up for the arrival of the confederate, who would excitedly tell of having come into possession of a large amount of money. Sometimes it would be an inheritance, or her late husband's insurance, or a purse found on the street. Whatever the details, the pigeon would always be promised a share of the money, since she, inadvertently, had been informed about it. All that she would have to do was prove herself trustworthy by putting up some large amount of cash as security until certain details could be taken care of.

One of the girls would stay with the pigeon while she went to her bank and withdrew what often was her life's savings. Turning over the cash to her new acquaintance, the pigeon would be told to be at a lawyer's office later that afternoon to receive her share of the money. "We always picked a real lawyer, just to make it look good," the ex–confidence woman said, "and we tried to find one that had his office on a top floor of one of the town's tallest buildings. That way it took the pigeon longer to get back down to the street once she found out there wasn't any split being made and that the lawyer never even heard of us. You'd be surprised how few of them ever went to the police—I guess they were ashamed to admit how they got taken."

I said that it was all too absurd. That no one would ever fall for such a transparent scheme. "Honey," the voice of experience said, "getting money out of people is the easiest thing in the world. All you got to do is promise them something they know they don't deserve. If there wasn't a streak of larceny in them, a stupid con like the pigeon drop couldn't work." Neither, I suppose, could some of the transparently false tactics that succeed at certain auctions.

Watching those well-dressed, carefully correct suburbanites bid for pressed ivory dust and cheap reproductions and new antiques, I found myself remembering the pigeon drop, and the ease with which seemingly sensible people let themselves be swindled.

The best way to make a killing at auction is to expect not to, while keeping alert for the opportunity when it can be done. But when comes the opportunity? Usually when you least expect it. At a small sale—so unimportant that the auctioneer did not bother to circularize his mailing list, because he did not think his regular buyers would be interested —we purchased a beautiful enameled lamp signed at the base and beneath the font by Joseph Gaspard Robert, who established the Marseilles porcelain manufactory in 1766. We had not gone looking for treasure, but we were able to bid it in at less than $50. The same auction yielded eight Lowestoft plates at one-sixth their value. Undoubtedly there are many auctions that are not worth attending, but if you are out to make a find, there are no auctions that are unworthy of inspection.

I know someone who bought a table that had been carved by Paul Gauguin. He didn't know that when he bought it for $20. Neither did anyone else at the auction, including the consignor and the auctioneer. Much later, when layers of grime and varnish had been removed, the incised signature emerged and the value of the piece skyrocketed. Since the buyer was then operating a small art gallery, he disposed of the table for an amount elusively described as "high five figures"—it being somewhat easier to be vague concerning private transactions than about prices at auction—and what we laughingly call "the twenty-dollar Gauguin" vanished into a limbo more luxurious than, but just as obscure as, that from which it had briefly emerged.

Certainly that was a killing, albeit an accidental one. The buyer, with no intent beyond decorating his gallery, had thought the carved table, stripped down and polished, might look nice near the entrance. It might hold, he thought, a potted plant and a rather important ashtray!

At what kind of auction was the Gauguin table found? A warehouse-storage sale! If it had been part of the estate of a well-known dealer or collector, it probably would never have squeaked by unnoticed. Not many killings are made at well-publicized auctions. Celebrity has its price, and not a few buyers are perfectly willing to pay accordingly. The "Hollywood auction," famous through the twenties and thirties, and again after World War II while the film industry gave America its nearest equivalent to royalty, capitalized on this. It is generally agreed that a minor piece in an important sale will command a substantially better price than it would bring in a less significant auction. You have a better chance to make a killing if you buy the best lot at a small sale. Of course, you will want to attend the "glamour" auctions. They're exciting, and fun. And an invaluable chance to learn. But don't expect to steal anything.

Occasionally you can find something among the cluttered pieces in a mixed lot—especially if it has been assembled from items unsold at some previous sale. At almost every auction a few lots will be passed. They may reappear lumped together in a single lot at the next sale. And because many buyers feel that nothing outstanding would be sold in a mixed lot, astonishingly good buys can sometimes be made. We once bought four beautiful old rose medallion demitasse cups in a mixed lot that went for $3—about one-twentieth of their value. Evidently our competitors were so busy ignoring the worthless glass and china that had been lotted in with them that they completely overlooked those beautiful little hand-decorated cups. (*See Chapter 7: How to Claim Your Purchases.*) We have found Vieux Paris pieces, Steuben crystal, Export Ware dishes, jeweled pillboxes, antique perfume bottles, sterling handles for canes and umbrellas, beaded evening bags and fine embroideries tucked away among the cracked china and chipped glassware in auction box lots. No killings, perhaps, but incredibly good values for the nominal prices we paid. Not every box lot yields such treasures. Many contain nothing but junk. And not infrequently, those lots into which one or two gems have mistakenly strayed will bring appropriately high prices. (I once found a Mettlach tumbler and a Gaudy Welsh teapot in an otherwise worthless box lot. Evidently several of my competitors also spotted those two desirable pieces, for the lot, much to the auctioneer's amazement, ultimately closed at $70 and set a pattern for fierce bidding that lasted throughout the sale.)

Some auctioneers are more generous than others when it comes to setting up mixed lots. "I prime it with one good piece," one auctioneer said, "and then fill it up with junk nobody'd bid for. It's the only way I can get some of this stuff cleared out." There is another gallery at which the box lots are so frequently desirable that I always examine them first when inspecting a sale. "Anything left unsold, or unclaimed, we lot it up and sell it the next time around," the manager told me. Most of the box lots at his sales bring between $10 and $30. Considering that the contents of one yielded items worth close to $300, they're remarkably good auction buys. Even steals.

With patience, one can sometimes acquire for a fraction of its worth a piece that has gone unsold through several auctions. Perhaps the first time, the auctioneer demanded too high an opening bid and the lot was passed. The second, he might have opened a bit lower, but failed to reach an established reserve. Subsequently, he might have arranged with the owner to sell the lot for whatever it would bring in order to satisfy his commissions. Or an item might appear at more than one sale simply because the auctioneer had been run-

ning a bid and been stuck with it. Then too, there are invariably lots that—although legitimately sold—go unclaimed because the buyer later realized he had overbid or overextended
himself, or for some other reason failed to complete the purchase.

I have seen repeated lots bring improved prices the second
time they were offered, but most often repetition diminishes
interest sufficiently to make possible a good—occasionally an
impressive—buy. If you regularly attend an auctioneer's sales,
you may find certain lots appearing with the predictability of
relatives who observe a birthday or a holiday visiting schedule.
Watch for them, and if they interest you, keep tabs on the
bids they bring. The lot that you lose at one sale might be
yours for much less at the next! And if he has previously had
trouble with the lot, the auctioneer will probably be willing
to close the bid substantially lower than he might have hoped.

There are sales at which lots recur with such frequency
that the audience will greet their presentation with weary
sighs and complaints of "Oh, that again!" Or someone in
the audience will remark in a stage whisper, "I thought he
sold that last week for two hundred dollars." If you hear them,
chances are good that the auctioneer does too. And that he
will realize that he had better dispose of the lot as quickly as
possible, or be prepared to withhold it from sale for a while.

If he elects to sell, you might be able to make a stunning
purchase that night. I once won a beautiful porcelain covered
bowl at $40. Two weeks earlier, I had lost the same bowl
when I stopped bidding at $125. I don't know if the original
buyer failed to claim it, if my bid was being run, or if it had
been bought back for the owner. I never bothered to try to
find out. At $40 it was a steal, and I was much too pleased
with my purchase to worry about what had gone wrong to
make it possible. The bowl has been appraised at nine times

what I paid for it, which makes me feel it was worth waiting for.

Regional differences, current fads and trends, and the availability of reproductions all affect the prices at which auction lots can be bought, sold or stolen. Your opportunities to make a find will increase in accordance with your awareness of these factors. Certainly fine antique furniture will always find an appreciative buyer, however much temporary popularity bentwood and turn-of-the-century oak may gain and lose. The current bentwood-and-oak vogue has boosted prices to unrealistic levels that have no relation to the value of the pieces. At a recent auction, I saw an ornate bentwood cabinet sold for $250, while a beautiful English Queen Anne highboy brought only $300. At another sale, a Victorian oak table went for twice as much as a fine hand-carved antique mahogany bench.

Possibly because American pieces are almost untouchable, English antique furniture is now beginning to be appreciated in the American market. A well-made piece in good condition not only could give many years of enjoyment, but also might prove to have been a splendid investment. Properly cared for, it can only ripen to greater beauty and value. I can't imagine what the oak and bentwood pieces will bring in a few years, when today's "fans" turn their enthusiasm (and their money) elsewhere. If you want to make a killing buying furniture at auction, you will probably have to wait until you stumble across one of Mr. John Goddard's blockfront desks going unrecognized by all but you. While you are searching, you can make some excellent buys among the English pieces often found at auction.

Exquisite Oriental porcelains, superb glass, splendid bronzes, choice examples of the great European porcelains, fine Oriental rugs, important tapestries and paintings will never be worthless, even though we may read reports that *famille verte* is currently less popular—and consequently less expensive—today than it was a few years ago when it was prominent in several important collections. Fine works have always been appreciated: not because of their age—invariably those same works were appreciated when they were *new*, and for the same reasons—but because of their excellence.

Learn to recognize quality and craftsmanship. The look of excellence is more reliable than markings (which can be faked), or catalogue descriptions (which might be inaccurate).* That same look will help you avoid the reproductions that clutter the marketplace and sometimes wipe out the value of the original. Victorian art glass has been slavishly copied within the past two years. And authentic pieces that earlier would have realized hundreds of dollars at auction have sometimes gone begging while the dull and lifeless copies have been bid in by the unknowing at prices far greater than their worth. Meanwhile, the abundance of reproductions has caused conservative buyers to shun all but *signed* art glass. Which, in

---

* Stamps are the only auction commodity that is invariably guaranteed to be as described. I have heard that coin auctions are conducted under the same conditions, but I have attended auctions at which coins formed a part of the lots and were offered for sale without guarantee of authenticity. In France, auction purchases are protected for a period of thirty years, and within that time the buyer is assured satisfaction for incorrectly described lots. In the United States, except where the conditions of sale include such specific provisions as those of Parke-Bernet, which were given in Chapter 3, even the best-intentioned auctioneer legally can, if he chooses, refuse to refund the price of any purchase. At some auctions, jewelry is unconditionally guaranteed. At others, "ruby" can be used to describe a genuine ruby, a spinel, a synthetic ruby, or a piece of red glass. Also in Chapter 3, I mentioned an auctioneer who uses the word "genuine" to designate those jewelry lots that he absolutely guarantees. Anything not so described may or may not be real, but it definitely is unreturnable! Some auctioneers insist that descriptions such as "Louis XV" are properly used to designate style, and are not to be considered indications of authenticity. "Queen Anne" will be used in some catalogues for any piece of furniture having cabriole legs. "Antique Queen Anne," however, would assign the piece to the eighteenth century. To bid intelligently, one obviously needs to learn to read between the lines in the catalogue and, perhaps more importantly, to recognize the line of genius, beauty, fine workmanship and value.

turn, has led to reproductions' being signed by various techniques ranging from careless scratching to careful engraving with a dentist's drill. Authentic pieces have been given spurious signatures. Copies have been given forged signatures. Catalogue copy and auctioneers' descriptions skirt the issue with words like "type," and "style," and "marked," and "attributed to," and (my favorite) "probably . . ." Rely instead on the evidence of beauty. On the perfection of detail, the fineness of design. On purity and vitality of color. It is a little like love at first sight, and at first glance it can be almost as misleading. And as exciting. And—occasionally—as rewarding.

Pseudo-experts will rattle off the date marks on Chinese porcelains and nod sagely and bid accordingly, while the connoisseur will judge the piece by its shape, its color, the style of decoration, the look and feel of the paste, the fineness of execution. He knows that reign marks may not be reliable. That later pieces frequently were signed with earlier dates in honor of the particularly fine achievements of that period. He also knows that auction catalogues sometimes throw around words like Sung and Ming and K'ang Hsi as casually as if they were scattering grain before a flock of chickens.* And that while it is fun to be able to recognize the various *nien hao*, they are, at best, a capricious guide.

In your eagerness to make a spectacular auction buy, don't assume that just because an item looks exactly like a picture

* Such pieces—whether or not they are genuine—never sell for chicken feed. If you want to make a killing, watch for the authentic piece that will come to the auction block with no more glorious designation than "old Chinese," or simply "Oriental." As long as you don't let yourself be overwhelmed by shop marks or signatures, you might have a chance to make an exciting buy. Look carefully, however, for any signs of mutilation. Many beautiful—and otherwise valuable—pieces have been drilled through for conversion into table lamps. If decorative value is your only concern, this might not greatly diminish your pleasure in the piece, but if you are expecting to make a killing, it would be wise to remember that, with rarest exceptions, any mutilation substantially reduces appraisal value. (*See Chapter 3: How to Inspect an Auction.*)

in a book, it must be authentic. Go to a museum and look at the real thing. If you can't find the same item, look at similar objects of the same period—if possible, by the same maker. *Don't* try to authenticate your auction find with a dealer, unless you plan to have the dealer act as your representative at the auction. For one thing, you might find him showing up there as your rival. For another, the gallery owner or antiques retailer, however much he might encourage browsing, is not running an information service. If his knowledge is extensive, it is undoubtedly based upon years of study and experience, and he rightfully should expect some compensation for sharing it with you. Dealers who will give you a quick, superficial opinion based on a verbal description or a catalogue photograph may only heap confusion upon misinformation. If you are out to make a killing, do your research at a museum.

And do it—like a good detective—privately. Word of a fabulous auction find spreads like a virus. The most unlikely people seem somehow to be able to sniff it out of the air. If you would have your killing remain yours alone—mum's the word! Use the library, the museum. Remember that even the most reputable shop will occasionally have a reproduction in its inventory. Bear in mind that recent auction records are a more reliable guide to value than the prices you might be quoted by a retailer—who may overquote because he expects to have to bargain down, or underquote in order to move an inferior piece. Then, if what you learned at the library or saw at the museum bears out what you thought at the auction exhibition, and you know that you are going to enjoy your find even if it proves to be worth less than a fortune, by all means go and bid for it.

Much of the potential pleasure of a fabulous auction find lies in sharing the news of your good luck and admirable shrewdness with others. If you have made a killing, and you would like to think that you might someday make a second, or a third, or a seventeenth: restrain your enthusiasm. There is a distinct enjoyment to be derived from telling someone that your $2 auction buy is actually worth $2,000. But remember that when you do, you automatically invite that person to bid against you for your next find. And even for routine lots that are not exceptional in any way. Once you bask in the glory of being a star buyer, any lot in which you are interested becomes of interest to those who have heard of your previous achievements. Continued success rests in anonymity. Where the competition is concerned, it is smart to be dumb. Let them feel sorry for you as you cart away your Gaudy Dutch dishes, your junky box lot with its one perfect signed bronze, your dusty old paintings of the Hudson River school, your Louis XV mirrors, your Ch'ien Lung jades, your . . . your . . . your . . . Smile, and say nothing, or suggest that perhaps you overpaid for "this old thing." Then, perhaps, you'll have a chance to make *another* killing.

6 HOW TO AVOID BIDDING AGAINST YOURSELF

"I THINK the auctioneer was running me up!" Who has not heard it? Which of us, for that matter, has not had occasion to say it? Nobody wants to give an increase on his own bid. He might be willing to overpay outrageously for a lot won in open competition with a legitimate rival, but he would bitterly resent having given an extra offer against a shill, or a phantom, or a phony "sealed bid." Letting an auctioneer trick you into bidding against yourself is foolish, widespread, frustrating and—unless you simply stop attending auctions—practically unavoidable.

Because it does happen. At some of the best auctions, and at some of the worst. And at almost every level in between. Bids are run smoothly or crudely, subtly or with an almost defiant invitation to challenge.*

* "Are we asking who's bidding, now?" one auctioneer, who is a notorious runner, demanded when a curious customer asked who it was that had bid against him. "Certainly not," the bidder replied, several shades less hostile than the auctioneer had been. "I merely wondered who had bid a hundred sixty, since I had neither seen nor heard the offer, and had thought the lot was mine at a hundred fifty." The auctioneer blanched. The customer, who happened to be one of America's most famous antiques dealers as well as a celebrated auction buff, patiently gave the next advance, and the lot—a fine Chippendale chair—was quickly knocked down to him at $170. The dealer knew perfectly well that he was giving an increase on his own bid, and by letting the auctioneer know that he was aware of the situation, managed to secure the piece without being taken

If an auctioneer is determined to run your bid, there is not very much that you can do to prevent it. He has countless techniques to fall back on—anything from plants and shills present in the audience to phony order bids, false consignor's reserves, and phantom bidders making invisible offers from the back of the house. Some of these tactics are almost pathetically easy to identify. Others blend effortlessly into the pattern of the sale and pass unnoticed either by all or at best by all but the most closely attentive. Certain auctioneers will try to run the bid on every lot that is introduced. Others will restrict themselves to certain important items, or to certain easily influenced customers. Most auctioneers quickly recognize a buyer who can be led into a bidding situation. A really

---

any further. Considerable authority is required to succeed with this stratagem. If you are absolutely confident that you can carry it off effectively, you might be able to use it *once* with an auctioneer. He could surprise you by treating you extremely well after that. Or he could suggest (or insist) that you retire from the bidding, and that if you return, he will not sell to you. Don't just assume because you cannot see or hear a bid that there is no legitimate competition. Many bids are given by advance order, and many by covert and often highly complex signals prearranged with the auctioneer. At some major sales it is unusual to see one hand raised in the course of the evening. Winks, nods, gestures with handkerchiefs, glasses, neckties, coats—those are the ways of the rich and mighty when they go out to buy at auction. One famous auction story involves a man of great wealth and distinction who did not wish to be recognized as a contender for a particular work of art that he wanted to buy. Before the sale began, he told the auctioneer of his interest and said that as long as he was wearing his overcoat, he should be considered to be actively bidding. The lot opened high and quickly surpassed the maximum offer the customer was prepared to give. With a sigh of resignation, he removed his overcoat, and watched dejectedly as the bidding continued. At last, finding the situation unendurable as the price climbed higher and higher, he rose, put on his overcoat and started to leave the gallery. He was shocked, thereupon, to learn that the lot was his— at several times the sum he had set as his limit. In the dispute that followed, he was told that inasmuch as he had been wearing his overcoat when the bidding closed, a final offer, naturally, had been accepted from him. Another famous buyer once devised a set of signals so complex that as the auction progressed both he and the auctioneer became so confused that midway in the sale the elaborately structured code had to be abandoned in favor of the less subtle but more readily recognized raised hand. Since some less-famous buyers seem to feel that covert bidding bestows a certain cachet, it is always possible for a legitimate bid to be invisible. Be sure an auctioneer is bluffing before you try to outbluff him.

skillful operator will even be able to predict, within a few dollars, just how far his customer will go. Other auctioneers, lacking that expertise, will close a sale with many unsold lots as evidence that they did not know when to stop running a bid.

Oddly enough, the most flagrant running is frequently found at the most insignificant sales. An auction involving important lots will usually attract sufficient interest to make bid running unnecessary. Perhaps the auctioneer will try to squeeze one or two additional advances out of a particularly lively or gullible buyer. Or will take bids from the consignor, if a lot is in danger of closing substantially below its true value. But for the most part, a major sale will inspire the kind of genuine competition that auctioneers sometimes choose to simulate.

One auctioneer, whose weekly sales seldom include any lots of outstanding quality—it being virtually impossible for a small gallery to assemble a sufficient number of first-rate items every seven days, even with the support of whole-salers' inventories and consignments from neighborhood re-tailers—habitually runs every bid, even if a lot opens at $1. If he does not receive an actual response to his asked-for open-ing, he will stare into a vague middle distance, frown slightly as if he did not quite comprehend some offer, pause for a moment and then ask, "How much?" Again he hesitates briefly, as if considering the bid. "All right," he will finally say, "I'll take it . . ." and the lot opens with an unheard, unseen offer from an invisible bidder. That this happens fre-quently, and on lots of no particular significance, confirms that he is not dealing with legitimate, but covert, offers. Understandably, the elusive patron who gives those mysterious opening bids wins many of the lots at those sales.

It is easy to know when one is bidding against that useful phantom. For one thing, the auctioneer—audacious as he is about running bids—does not quite have the nerve to take regular increments when there is no genuine competition. He will ask a $2.50 advance on a $10 opening when he sees more than one bid in the audience. But when he is taking bids out of the air, he will frequently accept an increase of $1 on a lot that opens at $25. Occasionally, having run the bid to a satisfactory level, he fails in his attempt to squeeze yet another dollar out of his customer. "Weren't you bidding?" he asks his invisible bidder. "Well, I thought you held up your hand!"—whereupon he will promptly knock down the lot to the under bidder who had previously refused to give a further advance.

When he first originated these weekly sales, this auctioneer protected his merchandise by announcing secured bids on all but the most ordinary lots. After his customers consistently failed to offer any advance on his "secured bids," he began taking bids out of the air, and developing his seancelike routine in which unheard voices speak and unseen hands give advances. Obviously, the secured-bid gambit closed the door to competition, while the introduction of an opening offer served to stimulate bidding. It is interesting to remember that while 75 percent of this auctioneer's lots were formerly protected by those "secured bids," virtually none of them now are. The phantom buyer—with whom the auctioneer holds occasional one-sided dialogues ("Do you want us to keep the piece up here? Yes, she wants it up here...."*) to which only he hears a response—has put an end to all that. The regular customers attend these sales faithfully, week after week, and although

---

* It is worth noting that "she" never wants anything delivered to her seat—as certainly she should not, since she is not there to accept it: even jewelry and small fragile items that any legitimate buyer would want to receive immediately. One way of identifying a shill, real or imagined, is by his unwillingness to accept small or valuable lots at auctions where purchases are delivered during the sale. Watch, too, where the questionable lots are placed as they are removed from the block. Frequently, you will notice them quite distinctly separated from items that were actually sold.

many of them are aware of the absurd little drama in which they are participating, they are apparently unwilling to let it interfere with their fun. Eventually, I suppose, they will realize that they are able to buy less and less as the auctioneer becomes increasingly shameless in his running. After a year, he will either have developed an entirely new audience or gone in search of one by moving his sales to a new location.

That is the solution that one spectacularly unethical auctioneer had to adopt. For some time, he regularly used two obvious shills. One sat up front and bid on all the low-priced lots. The other sat at the back and bid in anything expensive. It was the auctioneer's custom, as each lot was sold, to deliver it to the buyer. And he actually had his assistants carry every piece to the appropriate shill, who, in turn, carefully wrapped each item and packed it away. If it had not been that both of these men bought an incredible amount and variety of merchandise, we might never have suspected that they were there only as employees of the house. They carried off their part of the act extremely well, except for one important detail: neither of them ever bothered to record the lots he purchased, or the amounts he had paid.*

* There *may* be legitimate auction buyers who do not record each lot they win. That I have yet to meet any does not preclude the possibility that they exist. But if you suspect that a particular buyer is bidding for the house, watch to see if he keeps a record of his purchases. If you want to be doubly certain—so that you might not bother to attend another of that auctioneer's sales—wait to see if the suspected shill ever actually settles his account. If purchases were delivered during the sale, notice whether or not his are taken with him. Of course, some auction managements allow accounts to be settled within days, or even weeks, after a sale. In which case, your best confirmation will be the repetition of certain lots at subsequent auctions. If a lot that you wanted happened to be knocked down to a shill, you might try asking the auctioneer to buy it back for you. Tell him that you noticed Bidder So-and-So made many purchases and that in case he wanted to be relieved of that particular lot, you would be prepared to buy it for the amount of the next advance. Some auctioneers will go along with this; others will indignantly refuse. It is necessary to proceed with tact. You are, in a sense, suggesting that you know the sale was rigged, but if you make that too obvious, the auctioneer, however much he might want to make the sale, might have to refuse your request in order to save face.

By the end of the sale, it was evident that perhaps fifty out of two hundred and fifty lots had actually been sold and that the rest, as a result of unsuccessful running, had been knocked down to the two shills. Of course, that same merchandise formed the basis of that auctioneer's next sale. And his next. And his next. Each week he would legitimately sell a few of the leftover lots and add one or two new things to his basic collection. He switched shills, too. And numbers—although it became easy to know which numbers were the house accounts because they always stood somewhat apart from the series of numbers assigned to legitimate customers. The sudden appearance of 96, when all other bidding numbers ranged from 1 to 30, would immediately arouse suspicion. Initials were a little harder to identify, except from the bidding pattern (or, more correctly, the lack of rationale for bids), until one noticed that the person buying with the presumed shill's initials always sat alone.* Eventually, of

* Very few shills attend auctions in the company of wives, husbands, dates, friends, etc. Certainly there are sales at which the majority of the audience consists of unaccompanied individuals—midweek afternoon auctions particularly, when most of the buyers will be dealers. But on weekends, or at any evening sale, and most reliably, at suburban and country auctions, the solitary buyer will frequently be the one who is buying for the house. Dealers, who are there on business, may attend alone, but you will notice them greeting each other, sitting together, swapping stories, or exchanging opinions—in none of which a shill will usually get involved.
    I do know one professional shill who usually takes his wife and daughter along as a kind of camouflage. Like the old circuit riders, he makes the rounds of auctions in his neighborhood, sometimes helping out as handler or bid caller, but more often sitting down front and letting the auctioneer take bids from him whenever genuine competition fails to produce a satisfactory price. If he were more careful in scheduling his appearances, he would have gone undetected much longer, but he works with equal enthusiasm for the most obviously unethical auctioneers as well as for the more skillful operators, and after seeing him fill so many roles at so many different sales, it came as no great surprise to legitimate buyers to discover that among them was his not particularly admirable service as shill. Undoubtedly, at auction sales throughout the country, he has counterparts. Like him, they will probably reveal themselves to any careful observer.
    Most shills eventually give themselves away—if only by winning the majority of lots at every sale they attend. Every legitimate buyer will have an occasional

course, the auctioneer lost his audience. People grew tired of seeing the same lots "sold" week after week, particularly when they realized that however high they were prepared to bid, the house would usually enter one more offer against them.

The auctioneer moved to a nearby town and carefully omitted his name from the advertisements for his new sales. Most of those who had tried to buy at his previous auctions walked into the gallery, took one look, and promptly walked out. After a few weeks, the auctioneer adopted another tactic. He began holding his auctions on the premises of old houses, again advertising his sale without identifying the auctioneer, or else employing a fictitious name. Those who had not tried to buy from him before now went through the same frustrating routine. Some of them even returned the following week. Soon the auctioneer found that he had exhausted the potential audience in the area, and was obliged to hold his sales in another town.

Oddly enough, one was sometimes able to buy extremely well at his auctions. It was a bit like bathing in a crocodile pool—if you didn't keep your wits about you, you could come out missing an arm and a leg. But with patience and a sense of detachment, if not of humor, a good buy could be made. It sometimes happened that, having sold almost nothing for several weeks, he would, with desperate irrationality, suddenly knock down a lot on a ridiculously low bid. The next week, reverting to his usual routine, he would be impossible to buy from.

Once his shabby strategies have been fathomed, the auctioneer who persists in bidding against his customers seems either boring, comical, or infuriating. If you can enjoy his sales as the staged events that they are, you can have a fairly good time and even make an occasional purchase. You may

big day. Shills have them every time out. Eventually, most of us will attend a sale at which we win nothing. Very few shills can make that statement.

not buy very much unless you consistently overpay for the things you want. But if you are willing to bid fairly in what is a basically unfair situation, and you refuse to let the auctioneer lead you beyond your previously established maximum bids, you cannot be too badly hurt, and you might have a few pleasant surprises.

Perhaps because they run bids on so many lots, some of the most dishonest auctioneers make a point of giving several fast knocks in the course of every sale. (*See Chapter 4: How to Attend an Auction.*) This is not to suggest that any auctioneer who gives a lot a fast knock is also guilty of running bids. The fast knock is a legitimate technique used by many auctioneers to get attention and enliven the pace of a sale. The unscrupulous auctioneer, however, uses the fast knock to try to prove to his audience that his sale is absolutely on the up-and-up. If you can correctly judge when the fast knock is coming (seldom during the early or late lots at such a sale; but frequently one will immediately follow another as insurance that the desired point has been made), you can enjoy the satisfaction of having made a good buy at a sale where not many good buys were made. Provided, of course, you don't cancel out your gain by letting the auctioneer run you up on some subsequent lot that turns out to be less valuable than you thought.

Interestingly—though not, I suppose, surprisingly—the auctioneers who are most notorious about running bids also seem to be those who give the most unreliable descriptions of the lots they put up for sale. In fact, if you notice that the auctioneer's descriptions greatly exaggerate the value of a lot, or contradict what you found to be its condition, consider that an additional clue that the man on the platform might be inclined to bid you up.*

---

* Any auctioneer is liable to make an occasional mistake—to unintentionally overvalue a piece, or overlook some damage or repair. The men to watch out for

If you have discovered that an auctioneer—whether through a shill, or via a phantom bidder, or under the guise of a faked advance bid*—is your principal competitor, and you find the situation intolerable, your best response is to simply stop attending that auctioneer's sales. There *are* other auctions, you know. Try them. Your chances of finding an auction that you like, where you can buy successfully, are excellent. Thinking that you can persuade, or force, an unethical auctioneer to change his ways is liable to be frustrating, emotionally draining and costly in time and money. Fraud is an ugly word in any context. In an auction situation, it is also extremely difficult to establish. If the auctioneer holds a town, county or state license, you could ask the appropriate authority to investigate the manner in which business is conducted under that license. The effectiveness of your complaint will vary with the interest and aggressiveness of the agency and with the substance of your charge. Should you succeed in having his license revoked, you may be surprised to find the auctioneer officiating in some other capacity at the very next sale you attend. A representative of the Better Business Bureau reports that the Bureau, in his opinion, might best be able to serve as mediator between buyer and auctioneer, and would try to bring the two parties together and work out a solution satisfactory to both. How this approach, unfortified by legal pressure of any sort, would persuade an

---

are those who do this consistently. Some of their merchandise is as spurious as the phony bids they persist in entering for it. How appropriate, then, that they be left in possession of it.

* Although some auctioneers will simply have noted it on their lot list, a genuine order bid is usually carried on a separate sheet. If you observe the auctioneer referring to separate notes for certain order bids, you might be right to assume that others, not so noted, are somewhat less genuine. The auctioneer who uses the advance bid as a mask for running bids will usually give himself away by overusing it. Not often will advance bids have been left except on the more important lots in a sale. If prior bids are announced for many average lots, be on guard!

auctioneer to stop holding rigged sales is something I have not yet been able to figure out.*

His reputation is an important asset to any businessman. No auctioneer can hold successful sales once a majority of his audience becomes offended by his conduct. It seems a bit unfair to try to gauge integrity by the number of years a man has been conducting auctions in the same community, since that standard would tend to work against young men, or those who have recently come into the field, or those who, for nonbusiness reasons, have moved to a new town. Perhaps it would be better to suggest that if you know an auctioneer has been holding sales in the same area for several years, you can at least assume that, except for an occasional discreet squeeze, bid running is unlikely to be a problem.

If you cannot prevent an auctioneer from running bids, however, there are several things you *can* do to discourage him from running *your* bids. If the bidding seems to have resolved itself into competition with only one other bidder: look around† as if you were trying to identify the person bidding against you.

If you believe that your bid is being run, either because you recognize that your competitor is a shill or because you are convinced that there is no competitor, and you are willing to

* Provided the auctioneer chose to respond at all, the Better Business Bureau might be helpful in getting you a refund on a lot that you felt to have been misrepresented with regard to condition, performance, quantity, or authenticity. However, since even the most meticulously honest auctioneer will usually have protected himself with a blanket disclaimer relieving him of all such responsibility —look in the catalogue, or read the posted conditions of sale, or listen to the auctioneer's opening announcement: it'll be there—the Better Business Bureau's ability to obtain satisfaction for you will depend on the auctioneer's willingness to grant it. In which case you could probably have achieved the same result from a personal approach.

† I know this directly contradicts the firm rule about keeping your eyes on the auctioneer once you have entered the bidding. Which proves, I guess, that to every firm rule there are exceptions. Besides, if the auctioneer *is* bidding you up, there's not a chance in the world that he will take the bid away from you.

surrender the lot: stop bidding immediately. It is, in fact, a good idea to lose an occasional bid in order to indicate to the auctioneer that you are not the kind of compusive buyer who abandons all reason once he has entered the competition. Some men are particularly aggressive about winning. They bid at auction with a kind of fiercely competitive determination that suggests that their skill, power, wealth and virility are being tested. These men leave themselves open to the most obvious manipulation by auctioneers willing to exploit that competitive drive. Letting yourself lose an occasional lot is a good investment in a sensible auction image. It can save you a lot of money at those times when something you *are* determined to have regardless of the cost is placed upon the block.

When a lot that you do not want to lose is about to be offered by an auctioneer you suspect of trying to run your bids, walk to the back of the audience—be sure to stand where the auctioneer can see you, and where your view is equally unrestricted—and stand there while that lot is sold. Don't think the auctioneer won't realize what you are doing. He still may try to pull an extra bid or two from you, but your ability to observe the competition will discourage him from getting giddy about it. If the rear of the room is crowded with people milling about and seems an inauspicious place from which to bid, try standing at the front of the room, near the auctioneer's platform, or well forward to one side—again, provided you will be situated where the auctioneer can see your bids as well as you can see those that may, or may not, be entered against you. Some auctioneers will not permit you to stand down front. Some audiences won't either! Be sure to take your place immediately before the lot that you want is introduced. Act in a purposeful way. The whole bit is wasted if the auctioneer thinks you just got up to stretch, or to work out a muscle cramp.

If you have lost an important lot because the auctioneer

has persisted in running your bid, it is sometimes worthwhile to make a dramatic and somewhat indignant exit. Dramatic and somewhat indignant—and *silent!* If you leave muttering curses and imprecations, you weaken the effect of your grand moment—and, not incidentally, make it awkward for you to return to the next sale. Since being able to buy successfully at the next sale is the reason for your little scene, you do not gain by lousing it up with dialogue.*

You may be surprised to find how effective your bidding becomes at the next sale. Especially if you have formerly been a good customer. The auctioneer still may try to kite an occasional bid, and you may or may not have to resort to another walkout. If you do, play it cool, as if you held all the aces. If it gets to be an emotional thing with you, you risk coming to be thought of as a crank, or a hysteric.

If you see the lot that you lost introduced at a later sale, offer half what you previously bid, or half the auctioneer's opening demand. Try not to give the first offer unless it appears that the lot will be passed if you do not. Make no comment on the piece, and if the auctioneer chooses to favor the audience with some little story explaining how he happens to have the same lot again, try not to smirk or otherwise be observably knowing about it. If you are able to buy the piece for much less than you previously bid, you will have enough to smile about.

One way to encourage others—including the auctioneer— to bid against you is to discuss those lots for which you plan to bid. Some people think that by expressing their wants,

---

* Do not, however, get so carried away by your performance that you fail to stop to reclaim any deposits you may have given. If you have made previous purchases, it is dramatically effective to refuse to accept them, but it is not legally defensible. If your purchases include lots you would like to keep, try returning at the end of the sale to pay for and claim them. It is not unheard of that a dissatisfied customer and an auctioneer have straightened out such "misunderstandings" subsequent to the sale.

they can effectively discourage competition. That is foolish. So is telling the auctioneer how much you would like to have such-and-such, and just what you would do with it once you got it home. Involving the auctioneer in discussions of how you would have it reupholstered, refinished, rewired, cut down, built up, turned inside out, or whatever, only indicates to him how determined you are to buy it. Blame yourself if he later tempts, teases, cajoles, threatens, flatters, insults, bluffs, charms, shouts, begs, weeps, or otherwise tricks you into raising your own bid. To bid and buy wisely, know what you want, and see that nobody else knows.

Do not think that by deprecating the lot when it is put up for sale, you will reduce the price. Audibly observing that something is broken, incomplete, repaired or otherwise less than perfect will only serve to confirm your considerable interest in the lot. It is important that you know the true condition of the lot and that you determine your bid accordingly. But pointing out some defect, far from diminishing the price, will simply convey your intention to bid. Auctioneers know this, and some of them will apply that knowledge to your disadvantage. Competitors know it, too. And anyone seriously interested in bidding for the lot will also have observed its condition and will have adjusted his bid accordingly. You won't be telling him anything new. Additionally, your bid, following your initial reservation, substantially contradicts its effect. All you will have done is signal your interest to the auctioneer. He might then decide to run your bid, if only to indicate how desirable the lot really was. "The minute they sing out how there's a chip, or a hairline, or a finial missing or something," one auctioneer told me, "I know right off they want it, and most of the time I can get them to give a good price for it, too."

Bids from shills and other false competitors usually come immediately after genuine bids. If your competitor's bid is declared without hesitation, almost before your bid has been accepted, you might consider—particularly if the bidding has reached a fairly high figure—whether or not a genuine bid would be given so quickly. Are you hesitating? Have you already gone one or two bids beyond your preferred purchase price? Would any legitimate competitor perhaps try to reduce the advance? Wouldn't he at least hold back for a second, even as you pause to decide if you want to give the next bid? If he does not, then either he is determined to have the lot no matter how high he has to bid, or he is bidding for the house. Either way, if you have exceeded your previously determined maximum offer, you will do well to retire. It is pointless to bid against a demon. And it is foolish to bid against yourself.

Occasionally, when genuine competition is active, an auctioneer will achieve additional increases by taking an imaginary advance before acknowledging the next real bid. For example: if you are offering $30, the auctioneer will bypass your bid, pretend to take the $30 bid elsewhere and accept your bid at $40, or whatever would be the next increment. If you are confident that this kind of bid sandwiching is being used against you: speak up. Announce that your bid was $30. The auctioneer may correct himself. Or he may insist that he took someone else's bid at $30, and yours at $40. It is your privilege—and perhaps your best defense—to withdraw your bid at that point. If the competition was genuine, you will probably have an opportunity to reenter the bidding. You also will have indicated to the auctioneer (1) that you closely follow the progress of the bid, (2) that you are not a good subject for running, and (3) that you expect your bid to be acknowledged in preference to that of a competitor. Of course, the auctioneer may refuse to give preference your way. If you wish to continue to bid, do it vigorously, so that the auctioneer's refusal to acknowledge your bid will not go unnoticed by the audience. At least he will be unable to continue to ignore you.*

An additional technique by which an unethical auctioneer can sometimes obtain more for a lot than was actually bid involves switching the basis on which a multiple lot was sold, so that the buyer, having bid *for the lot,* finds himself billed at that price *for each unit* of which the lot consisted. Your best defense against this kind of kiting is to know exactly how the lot is being sold (*See Chapter 4: How to Attend an Auction*), to listen closely to any declaration that the auctioneer makes at the time he offers it, to carefully analyze your itemized bill before you pay it, and to respond immediately at any point along the way at which such a switch becomes apparent. At some auctions, the conditions of sale specifically state that unless otherwise noted, any bid for a lot consisting of more than one item shall be an offer for only one item in the lot. Don't blame the auctioneer for your failure to have taken note of such a provision. On the other hand, don't, as I once saw someone unprotestingly do, pay double for a lot that, having been sold by the pair, was billed on a per-piece basis. And don't be so stunned that you fail to speak up if, as he knocks down a lot to you, the auctioneer switches your bid to a per-unit offer. Set the matter straight immediately. If the switch was unintentional, the auctioneer will probably apologize and correct his records. If it was deliberate, he may elect to resell the lot, in which case you will at least be able to bid in accordance with the manner in which you can expect to be charged.

---

* He might refuse to sell to you. Or if you make a real nuisance of yourself, he might ask you to leave. If he does, you have little to gain by attending his next sale, unless you have used the time between auctions to straighten out the situation.

7 HOW TO CLAIM YOUR PURCHASES

TWICE IT has happened to us—and considering the number of auctions we have attended, that may not seem particularly alarming, but twice is exactly two times too many to have been refused delivery of an auction lot that one has bid in and for which payment has been given.

In Chapter 5, I mentioned the lovely old rose medallion cups that we won in a $3 lot of mixed china. We had made several other purchases at that sale. At the end of the day, we paid our bill, which listed the various lots, and presented it for delivery. Shortly, we received all of the items except the cups. I asked for them, and was told that they could not be located. I pointed out that according to the rules governing the sale —rules clearly set forth in the auction catalogue, as it happened—ownership of each lot passed to the buyer at the fall of the auctioneer's hammer. Since the cups had legally been my property for several hours, I suggested that either they be given to me promptly, or that I be allowed to go behind the delivery counter to look for them.

At that point, the auctioneer's wife assumed the role of *dea ex machina* and, descending into the middle of the situation, imperiously sought to resolve it by insisting that she intended to refund my purchase. I said that I did not want a refund, but expected delivery of my property without any further delay. Betty, meanwhile, went to find the auctioneer —who, unaware of the situation, immediately "found" the missing cups but, under his wife's sternly admonishing glare, promptly refused to deliver them to us. The cups, he said, were worth considerably more than we had paid for them and only a careless mistake had caused them to be lotted in with some worthless things that had sold for $3. We insisted that the lot had been on exhibition with the cups included, and that since we had so seen it at inspection, we had bid for it on that basis. We felt that the cups—lost or found—were ours and that the auctioneer's refusal to give them to us was equivalent to having them stolen.

The auctioneer then blandly suggested that we make a small additional payment to help offset the loss he had sustained by selling the cups for a fraction of their worth. In the argument that followed, each of us presented our views on the legal, ethical and financial aspects of the situation, while Mrs. Auctioneer, who, I later learned, is famous for her unpleasantness, favored us with her impression of the legendary basilisk.

I finally said that as far as I was concerned, Mr. and Mrs. A. were guilty of theft, and that I was going to call the police to make them relinquish the cups. While I went to telephone, Betty suggested that in addition to the police, we would be anxious to tell the local newspapers exactly what had happened. The auctioneer evidently felt that bad publicity was a greater threat than any possible intervention by the local authorities, for he quickly wrapped the cups and, with his wife's crestfallen help, carefully packed them and delivered them to us.*

---

* Though silent, the auctioneer's crew took obvious pleasure in our victory. Our fellow buyers, however, who witnessed our minidrama while claiming their purchases, behaved as if we had just donned leper's bells. About two years later, we happened to attend another sale conducted by this auctioneer and his still

The second such incident involved a lot consisting of nine pieces of glass. Six of the items were of negligible value. The remaining three were a Bristol vase that we did not want; an etched stein of considerable beauty, but having a repaired handle; and a signed Steuben *verre de soie* vase decorated with threads of blue Aurene. I had inspected the lots two days in advance of the sale and had noted the Steuben item as a possible find. After we had won the lot with a $22 bid, we were given the six negligible pieces, the Bristol vase and the repaired stein. When we asked for the ninth piece, we were told that the lot had been changed and that we had received everything included in it. This happened at the close of the first session of a three-day auction. The auctioneer pointed to a lot that would be going up on the final day. "Is that the vase you're talking about?" he asked. We said that it was and that at the exhibition it had been one of the nine pieces in the lot for which we had bid.

The auctioneer said that the vase had not been displayed on the block at the time the lot was sold. That was true. But then neither had several of the other items. The catalogue described the lot as consisting of nine pieces of glass, and the auctioneer had so introduced it. Our paid receipt called for nine pieces. There had been no mention of a change in the makeup of the lot from the way it had been shown at the exhibition. We asked the auctioneer why he had not announced the withdrawal of one item from the lot. "We don't have to do that," he said, thrusting the traditional disclaimer

formidable wife. We could not tell if they remembered us. Certainly they gave no indication of it. Maybe the experience—remarkable as it was to us—was everyday business to them. That might explain why the crew had seemed especially gratified by our determination and success. And why the customers resented our challenging a stratagem to which they themselves might previously have surrendered. Mr. and Mrs. Charm-and-Audacity might long ago have changed their ways if more buyers had insisted that the auctioneer as well as the audience is bound by the rules governing a sale.

concerning authenticity, condition, quantity, etc., under my nose.

I pointed to the repaired stein. "Suppose I had failed to notice that this piece was damaged," I said, "and overbid for it? Wouldn't I have to accept it?" The auctioneer nodded. "That's why you have things on exhibition, isn't it?" I asked, a little pleased with myself for having come up with what I thought to be a clever bit of strategy. "That's right," the auctioneer said. "Then why," I insisted, "isn't the converse true? Why isn't the exhibition also held to establish how *good* the lots are?" I pointed out that I had inspected a lot consisting of nine pieces, that the catalogue called for nine pieces, that the lot had been presented as nine pieces, and that our bill specified nine pieces. "And *that*," I said, dramatically pointing to the locked cabinet where the Steuben vase was shelved, "is the ninth piece, and I want it delivered to me without any more of this nonsense."

The auctioneer smiled blandly. "You don't think we're going to let a piece like that go on a twenty-two-dollar bid, do you?" he asked. His tone suggested that if I did, I was being somewhat shamelessly naive. He reached into a box lot and removed a cheap pink glass ashtray. "Here," he said. "You want nine pieces of glass? This is number nine."

I repeated that I wanted the ninth piece that I had seen on exhibition in the lot. When he replied that he was not going to give it to me, I called upon my memory of the incident of the rose medallion cups and immediately said that I had plenty of good contacts with the press and would see to it that his gallery got an avalanche of unpleasant publicity. The auctioneer seemed singularly unimpressed. He muttered something nasty about libel. Then Betty decided that perhaps the police should be summoned. Not because we expected them to do anything, but because we wanted to convince the auctioneer that we were determined not to be laughed off, or intimidated.

The police came, and rather indulgently suggested that Small Claims Court was the proper place for our complaint to be heard. But taking the auctioneer to court would have given us no satisfaction whatsoever. For one thing, our vase would have been sold long before our case could have been heard. We might have recovered our $22, but that was not what we really wanted. Finally I said, "If you refuse to deliver to me the contents of the lot that I purchased, exactly as shown at exhibition, I am going to report you to the Commissioner of Licenses. Plus which, I will personally picket this gallery, and with signs and handbills, I'll tell every one of your customers just how you run this business. And if you have the nerve to put that vase up for auction, I'll report you for selling stolen property, because as far as I am concerned, that vase became mine the minute your gavel fell and title to that lot passed to me."

The auctioneer frowned. "Well," he said, "I am going to sell that vase on Saturday. But I'll buy it back myself, and if you come in on Monday, I'll have it for you. But I'll appreciate it if you don't attend any more of my auctions. And if you have the nerve to, don't expect that I'll sell to you, because I won't."

I had made so many different appeals and threats that I never was able to decide which had been the effective one. The end of the story is that we did return on Monday, did receive the Steuben vase and the remainder of our purchases, and, finding that the auctioneer kept his word to that degree, have not bothered to test his other pledges. I have since heard it said that this auctioneer is achieving a reputation for unreliability. That articles bought from him have been found to have been misrepresented. Which confirms my feeling that we are not missing very much by honoring his request that we not attend his sales.

If, when you go to claim your purchases, you are told that a lot on which you feel you have made an exceptional buy has been broken, lost or otherwise made undeliverable, do not be too quick to accept an offered refund.* If you are told that your purchase has been broken, ask to see the pieces. If this is treated as an extraordinary request, suggest that you would like to be able to consider the feasibility of having repairs made. Do not be too easily put off by ridicule. If you are told that all fragments, parts, whatever, have been swept up or thrown into the garbage, ask to see the sweepings, or the garbage cans. For one thing, you actually might want to have the piece restored. For another, you at least can be certain that the damage did occur and was extreme. If you are told that your purchase has been lost, ask to be allowed to help look for it. If you are not permitted into the storage area,† wait until all other buyers have claimed their purchases, if only to get a look at what has been left.

* Most auctioneers disclaim responsibility for broken, lost or stolen merchandise, which, once it has been sold, is handled at the buyer's risk. They may or may not elect to give you a refund, or to make allowance for some minor damage. You will not often be offered a full refund on a lost or broken item. Instead, the auctioneer will probably want to discuss an adjustment, or will offer to pay for or contribute to the cost of repairs, or will suggest that you make a claim under his insurance policy. He might ask you to be patient and give him a few days to recover a lost item, after the majority of the lots in the sale have been delivered. He may tell you that your purchase has been given to another buyer, and that he is confident he will be able to correct the mistake within a day or two. If he does agree to a refund, he might first offer it to you in the form of credit against future purchases.

Of course, you must not assume that an auctioneer is dishonest if he suggests a full cash refund. Maybe he's just a remarkably decent, generous and fair individual. In which case, he will not be reluctant to show you the broken pieces, or let you assist in the search.

† Plenty of good reasons why you should not be. Including the need to protect other purchases from damage, or theft. And to protect you from possible injury as large or heavy articles are being moved about. As one auctioneer put it, "to keep you from breaking anything, and anything from breaking you!"

Breakage does occur. Pieces do get lost. But not very often. Ask yourself how long an auctioneer could continue in business if he repeatedly had to make good for damaged or missing items. Even the most ill-trained crew will exercise maximum care in handling customers' merchandise. And if it is suggested that your purchase was mistakenly delivered to another buyer, it stands to reason, doesn't it, that there would be an unclaimed lot left to compensate for it?*

If you are refused delivery of all or any part of a lot for any reason whatsoever, hold your ground and insist on satisfaction. Any reputable auctioneer will want to do whatever he reasonably can to see that you have it. Those few disreputable ones deserve the consequences of any drastic course they force you to pursue. Don't, however, get so carried away that you forget that the auctioneer probably cannot in any event, be held liable for more than the purchase price of the lot. Your purchase might be worth $10,000. but if you paid only $10 for it, *that's* about all you can expect to recover.†

Occasionally a piece that was perfect, or showed only a minor defect, at the time of inspection will be delivered in less desirable condition. If you are positive that the damage was not present, or was less severe, when you saw the lot on exhibition, ask the auctioneer for an adjustment or, if it seems in order, for a full refund. Be sure, however, that the flaw is not something that you failed to notice when inspecting the piece. If the auctioneer suggests that the best he can do is try to resell the piece for you, accept that offer only as a last resort. It is doubtful that he will be able to achieve a com-

---

* If there is, then tracing your lot should properly be classified as child's play, don't you think?

† "The highest bid shall in all cases be accepted by both the buyer and seller as the value against which all claims for loss or damage shall lie" is the way one auction catalogue phrases it. Others may put it differently—but, as we used to say of small gifts, it's the *thought* that matters.

parable price for it, particularly if he feels obliged to mention the defect responsible for your dissatisfaction.

One way to avoid possible damage or loss is to have each lot you purchase delivered to you as it is removed from the auction block. Obviously there are sales at which this is impossible. Equally obvious is the fact that there are certain lots for which, because of size or weight, immediate delivery is unsuitable. And if you make many purchases, you can quickly find yourself uncomfortably surrounded by a rising tide of cartons, newspapers and unwrapped pieces that threatens to crowd you out of your chair. If you are holding things, or busy wrapping them, it is difficult to raise your hand to enter a bid. And it is more difficult to make note of a purchase, to make a payment or deposit, and to accept change. It is a good idea, however, to have jewelry and other small, precious lots delivered to you immediately. If you are alone, though, remember that you will have to take any delivered items with you whenever you have occasion to leave your seat. Accordingly, you might want to take delivery only of those lots that will fit easily into your handbag or pocket, and ask to have any other items held for you until the conclusion of the sale.

The most common procedures for paying for and claiming auction purchases are:

(1) On arrival, bidders register with the bookkeeper. A bidding number or set of initials is assigned, and an advance deposit, applicable to all purchases, may or may not be collected. No purchases are delivered until the conclusion of the sale, when all buyers settle their accounts and claim their merchandise. In some instances, purchases are not delivered at the conclusion of the sale and must be called for on the following day, or within a specified period of time.*

---

* If you are traveling, or will travel to attend a particular sale, it is wise to telephone ahead to confirm that you can collect your purchases on the day of the auction. You might save a lot of time, mileage and trouble. Most of the auctioneers who institute this rule are earnest about not making exceptions to it.

(2) No merchandise is delivered until the conclusion of the sale. At the auctioneer's discretion, buyers may or may not be required to make deposits against their purchases as they win them. A cash man circulates through the audience, collecting deposits and issuing receipts. Bids are taken by name or initial, and buyers known to the house usually are not asked to secure their purchases with deposits.*

(3) No deposits are taken, although bidders are required to register on arrival. All merchandise is delivered to the buyer as it is removed from the block. Buyers can settle their accounts at any time during the sale and, having been given their purchases, are able to leave whenever they choose. Except that this sometimes causes some confusion in the audience—particularly if large items are being delivered or removed, and especially if the buyer happens not to be seated on the aisle—this is a dandy system. Thoughtful buyers will ask to have large pieces held aside for them. Not having a cash man wandering through the audience greatly expedites the sale, while being able to settle your account before the close of the auction saves you from having to stand in those long, irritating waiting lines.†

* You may be surprised and somewhat flattered to find that after you have bought at only one of his sales, the auctioneer will accord you this privilege. Yes, he does remember you and all of his other buyers from one auction to the next, and always will, even as he will remember your name, initials or bidding number after you have bid in only one or two lots a sale. Some auctioneers will remember what you bought and even—incredibly—some of the things you did not win. I once lost the bid on a Tiffany lamp when it started soaring into the thousands, but in spite of my early retirement, the auctioneer who handled that sale has me mentally filed away as a Tiffany buyer and, even though I have not subsequently bought or bid on a comparable lot, never fails to call when he has something similar going up for sale.

† If you know this system is being followed, go early and take a seat on an aisle. Try to sit in the first row if you plan to purchase many small items; near an exit if you will be buying furniture or other bulky or heavy lots. (Why? Because the handler delivering your purchases will bring them to your seat, and when you have to maneuver them out of the salesroom, you will be glad to have awkward items near an exit. On the other hand, sitting in the front row will give you room for cartons, paper and any other packing you need to properly

(4) All lots are delivered immediately, and paid for in full at the time of purchase. Which is what most—but not all—auctioneers mean by "cash and carry." The hundreds of individual transactions that take place in the course of a sale so conducted are seldom accomplished with perfect smoothness and accuracy. If you plan to make many purchases at such a sale, see if you can open an account with the book-keeper. If that involves having your purchases held until the conclusion of the sale, it might be worth that possible inconvenience. Invariably, the runner has to hand you the item you have won before he can receive your money. You, meanwhile, are holding your money (plus, perhaps, your notebook, pen, refreshments, other purchases) and cannot easily receive the item. For an awkward moment, you and the runner blankly look at each other. If you are lucky, a friendly neighbor will come to your aid and receive the piece for you, and hold it until you have settled the financial aspect of the transaction. Paying cash as you go does have the advantage of giving an instant account of your purchases. So does having each lot delivered to you.

It is important to know which of these payment and delivery procedures is being followed and with what special variations. How you will be able to claim your purchases will affect which auctions you want to attend and what you might want to buy. For example, you might think twice about bidding in some inconsequential lot if you know that you will have to wait through five hundred following lots in which you have no interest before you can pay for and receive your purchase. You also might consider letting a small lot go if you know that claiming it will involve another trip to a distant gallery.

---

store small purchases. Behind row one, you will sometimes barely have room for your feet!)

Except at cash-and-carry auctions, the one thing you will always need in order to claim your purchases is a PAID bill from the cashier. A properly prepared bill should record the lot number (unless lots were not sold by number); a description that sufficiently identifies the lot and includes any specific terms that would affect value or warranty;* the quantity, which should be consistent with the catalogue description or the auctioneer's declaration; and the amount of your bid, which should be *exactly* the same as that which you recorded. *Be sure that you find your bill to be correct in all respects before you pay it.* Any deposits that you have given should have been deducted from the total in determination of the amount due.

If you have any question about your bill, be satisfied with the answer before making final payment. Do not be afraid to ask. If you are reluctant to inquire about something because you do not want to hold up the cashier's line, then go to the back of the line and wait. Do not let your sensitivity, the cashier, or impatient people waiting to be served rush you into paying a bill with which you are not completely satisfied. If the cashier says that only the auctioneer can resolve a particular difference, *wait* until the auctioneer is available and straighten out the matter with him *before* settling your bill. If you want a particular assurance, or guarantee, obtain it in written form and have the auctioneer's signature on it. If possible, have it written on your bill. If that is impractical, then be sure that any separate certification makes reference to the bill number, the sale date and the lot number so that it is incontestably related to that purchase.

You will have kept a record of the numbers of the lots that you won, and the amount at which you purchased each of them. Check this against the cashier's bill, and make sure that

---

* Such as "sterling," if you bought it to be sterling. The name of the maker, artist, manufacturer or whatever, if that served as an inducement for you to bid.

they agree. Even if the total amount is correct, and you have received your purchases during the sale, do not accept an unitemized bill.* If you haven't been given your purchases during the sale, present your PAID bill to an attendant at the delivery station, and check the items that you receive against your list to be sure that you receive the correct lots, and that they are complete. Before either you or the attendant wraps anything, check that it has been delivered to you in the same condition in which you found it at the exhibition. If you have not tested the operation of a mechanical or electrical device, and it has been sold to you as being in running or working order, test it *before* you remove it from the premises.

Be sure that you have been given all the components of any article, and that delivery has included any promised accessories, such as keys, weights, pendulums, knobs, drawer pulls, escutcheons, bits of molding, handles, finials, shades, bases, ladles, stoppers, spreaders, spoons, tongs, forks, covers, table leaves, drawers, doors, shelves, locks, pegs, cases, linings, stands, snuffers, casters, etc. etc. etc. If you are told that although some such incidental came with your purchase, it has disappeared, but that a replacement can easily be bought for a few dollars at any hardware store, furniture shop, clock-maker's, antiques shop or whatever—suggest that you would prefer to have the promised element produced, and if that is absolutely out of the question, ask the auctioneer to replace

---

* Remote as it may seem at the time of purchase, there is always a possibility that you will want to return or resell something that you bought at auction. (*See Chapter 4: How to Attend an Auction.*) And if you needed to establish how and at what price you acquired something, you would have a difficult time of it if your receipt simply said that you had paid an aggregate amount for various unspecified lots. Save your auction bills. They are interesting to review from time to time, are useful in settling arguments and, should a question of proprietorship ever arise, can serve you better than a battery of attorneys.

it for you.* Unless you happen to be in a related field, the auctioneer probably has better sources for these things. Plus which, your approach might encourage him to search a bit harder to locate the original for you.

Wrap breakable articles in at least a double layer of paper, and pack cartons securely, filling any empty spaces with crushed newspaper. Separate elements should be wrapped separately, and then rewrapped or packed together. If you have many small pieces, wrap them individually and then combine them in a single package so that in unpacking you will not accidentally discard one of them.† If an attendant is packing for you, or helping you to pack, do not hesitate to ask him to be more careful, if you think he should be. Suggest that you prefer to do your own wrapping, if you feel it to be necessary. Ten to one, the attendant will be delighted to be relieved of the chore. An attendant who does a competent job of delivering your purchases and helping you pack them deserves a tip.‡

Large pieces can present problems. Things can look quite different on exhibition and on the auction block from the way they do when lashed to the roof of your car; and no

---

* Those easy replacements somehow never seem so simple once one enters the marketplace in search of them. Let's face it: if keys for all those banks, clocks, desks, trunks, cupboards and gum machines were so easy to find, all those other banks, clocks, desks, trunks, cupboards and gum machines would not keep showing up at auction without keys. The same could be said for other annoyingly elusive parts and pieces. Good luck with those "standard elements available anywhere." In my experience, most of them are about as plentiful as the legendary phoenix.

† All that careful packing is wasted if unwrapping is done carelessly, you know.

‡ Yes, he does. Probably because we are not accustomed to tipping for wrapping services in retail shops, we sometimes forget to reward similar services when we buy at auction. Be guided by the amount of time and effort he has spent helping you. Expect him to give you superb service at the next auction. Who doesn't appreciate a bit of appreciation? And if you have to ask for an extra-strong or outsize carton, some cord, tape, a screwdriver or a hammer, it is always helpful to have a friend at court.

matter how inexpensively some massive lot is sold, it might not represent such a bargain if delivery charges must be added to the price. Most auctioneers either have a long-established working arrangement with a truckman or will be able to recommend a delivery service for you. The ubiquitous trailer-rental agencies that dot the countryside can solve some delivery problems, provided: (1) you are not made uncomfortable by the idea—if not the reality—of this attachment to your car, and you will not be using roads on which such vehicles are prohibited; (2) equipment adequate for your purchases is available when you need it;* (3) your things will not be damaged in transit—consider the weather if you are going to be using an open vehicle; (4) you can handle unloading and placement when you reach your destination.

It is wise to anticipate any unloading problems before attempting to transport difficult-to-handle pieces. The length of clothesline and the old blanket that you keep in your car might serve perfectly well for getting a massive sideboard to your home, but in the event that you are not an experienced furniture mover, what will you do with that piece if it does not easily fit through the door? Caught up in the excitement of a sale, we seldom consider such possibilities—unless, of course, we have had occasion to cope with them before. Staggering up to your own front door in the lonely chill of the hour before dawn with only your wife to help you unload a marble-topped, mirror-backed monstrosity can make you wonder just what in hell you thought you were doing when you bought that old thing. It is a lesson not quickly forgotten!

Potential delivery problems, however, should never prevent one from taking advantage of a fabulous auction buy. If pro-

---

* Since agencies do not all maintain twenty-four-hour service seven days a week, it might be necessary to secure equipment before an auction. On the other hand, your effort and expense could be wasted if you fail to win the lot that you have prepared to transport.

fessional help seems to be in order, talk to the ever-present "truckman on premises."

Try to establish the truckman's fee in advance. If he is unfamiliar with the distance and unable to quote a flat rate for the job, agree on an hourly rate and try to set a maximum beyond which you will not be charged. Be sure that both you and he understand that his services will include establishing the pieces where you want them in your home. If this all seems too trivial, try to imagine yourself single-handedly maneuvering that old Victorian solid-oak whatever-it-is upstairs to wherever-it-was you had planned to use it. Now, wouldn't it have been better to have that part of it squared away even before the piece was loaded onto the truck?

You might save part of the truckman's fee if you find someone else at the auction who can share a delivery run with you. If your purchases and Mr. X's can be combined into a single load and delivered to the same address, or one set of purchases to an address that is directly en route to the other, you may be able to divide the cost of a single trip—plus, perhaps, a small additional charge for the extra stop.

Be sure that you establish a definite date and approximate hour when delivery will be made—and be sure that your goods will be removed from the auction site within the allowed time. Some galleries charge storage on purchases left longer than one or two days after a sale. Per diem charges of $2 on small items and $4 for larger ones are typical. They can add substantially to the cost of what you buy at auction. If you are going to be paying extra for delivery, it makes no sense at all to incur such additional charges.

If you are not going to be present when your purchases are picked up by the truckman, be sure that he has a written authorization listing the lots he is delivering for you, and see that the auctioneer knows exactly what arrangements you have made, including the name of the carrier, especially if you will be using a delivery service other than that with which the auctioneer usually works.

One of my favorite auctioneers opens every sale with a fast recitation of the rules, invariably closing with, "I hope you buy what you like, but even more, I hope you like what you buy!" Careful inspection and clever bidding will help you buy what you like at auction. Properly claiming your purchases and getting them safely home is the final step toward liking what you have bought.